ENDORS

This book is a treasure trove of insights, strategies, and best practices into what it takes to thrive and prosper as a leader in today's fast-paced and ever-changing workplace. The nine questions identified by Theurer and Jelks provide a practical, relevant framework for both emerging and seasoned leaders and the coaches who work with them. Their book strikes the perfect balance between self-reflection (which few of us do enough of) and thoughtful action. Read this wonderful book and share it with those you lead and mentor.

STEPHEN M. R. COVEY, #1 best-selling author of *The Speed of Trust* and coauthor of *Smart Trust*

The real challenge in health care will be the need for confidence, innovation, and creativity. We can only cultivate these attributes with a grounded awareness of who we are, what we stand for, and our vision for our organizations. *Missing Conversations* challenges us to hit the pause button, reflect on the key questions that are central to developing ourselves, and face into our challenges with renewed vigor. Whether you're new to leadership or a seasoned veteran, give this book your time and energy. You'll land on new insights, practices, and actions that make an immediate and positive impact.

JUDITH ROGERS, RN, MSN, PhD, President, Holy Cross Hospital

Missing Conversations is a pragmatic, accessible, thought-provoking guide to leadership that is useful for emerging leaders as well as veterans who need to recalibrate their vision, goals, talents, and humanity. The practices in this book move one to an in-depth self-reflection that opens to new actions and behaviors.

RICHARD STROZZI-HECKLER, founder of the Strozzi Institute, author of *The Leadership Dojo* and *The Art of Somatic Coaching*

Missing Conversations is an invaluable read for leaders of all perspectives as it provides us a practical map for reaching beyond the standard language of leadership and asks us to challenge our self-awareness—one of the foundational necessities but least exercised characteristics for strong leaders. Through a rich progression of provocative exercises and actions, Theurer and Jelks introduce us to a meaningful journey that will help us to become the leaders of substance we wish to become and our community needs us to be.

William F. Magner III, President,
U.S. Markets, Cushman & Wakefield

One of my most important responsibilities as an executive is to cultivate the potential of current and future leaders. *Missing Conversations* provides a practical yet substantive framework for leadership development. I will be sharing this book with many of the people I manage and mentor and recommend it to any leader who wants to become a more inspired and effective presence in their organization.

Patrick Connolly, COO,
Sodexo North America President, Sodexo Health Care

If you're a leader juggling multiple priorities and your time for reflection and development is limited, *Missing Conversations* is the leadership book to turn to for inspiration and guidance.

Ann Yerger, Executive Director,
The Council of Institutional Investors

Missing Conversations provides the guidance and tools that any leader, HR professional, or coach needs to be successful and satisfied. This is a rare book that will encourage you to pause and reflect and inspire you to take concrete actions to maximize your potential. Read it and share it with those who want to accelerate their careers!

Sharon Armstrong, PHR, CMF HR Consultant/Author
of *The Essential Performance Review Handbook, Stress-free Performance Appraisals,* and *The Essential HR Handbook*

Leadership comes from within—there are no boundaries that limit it to titles, professions, age, gender, or ethnic background. Anyone who responds to the wisdom in *Missing Conversations* and embraces self-reflection as a tool and acts on it will become more effectively engaged in every aspect of their personal and professional life. This book is a must-read for anyone who wants to make a positive difference in the world in which they live.

Vincent A. Wolfington, Senior Advisor, Gallup,
Former Chairman and CEO, Carey International

Theurer and Jelks's significant new contribution is a thoughtful exploration of nine important internal conversations. While they are real dialogues, they are all too easy to avoid. Aware leaders must face these central questions in service to their own development. Well-grounded in business examples, the book makes elusive material pragmatic and concrete. Filled with practical tools, assessments, and exercises, the book is rich yet accessible and productive. Coaches, too, will find this an invaluable resource for guiding significant developmental work for their leadership clients.

Doug Silsbee,
author of *Presence-Based Coaching*

I was immersed in this book from the beginning. The Missing Conversations Self-Assessment gave me immediate pause, enlightening me to the fact that there was much in my leadership approach that was reactive and impulsive rather than considered and reasoned. The real-life stories used by the authors made the concepts accessible. Any manager will find this book helpful in charting a course of action for becoming a more capable and confident leader.

Thomas J. Serena, Executive Vice President of
the American Gastroenterological Association

Organizations can be defined as "networks of relationships, conversations and commitments." If your organization isn't getting the results you want, one of the most important places to turn your attention to is the conversations you are having, or not having, as a leader. In *Missing Conversations*, Theurer and Jelks have identified which conversations or questions leaders need to reflect and act upon in order to thrive and prosper. We will be recommending this book in our Coaching Excellence in Organizations program and highly recommend it to any leader or coach who wants to inspire those they work with to achieve greater results.

Robert Dunham, co-author of *The Innovator's Way*

MISSING
CONVERSATIONS

9 Questions All Leaders Should Ask Themselves

Bridgette Theurer & Heather O'Neill Jelks

First published by Createspace

First Edition

611 N. View Terrace, Alexandria, VA 22301
Tel: 703-836-1571

Cover & Interior Design: StyleMatters, www.style-matters.com

ISBN-13: 978-1503269095
ISBN-10: 1503269094

To my husband, Doug, one of the most naturally gifted managers and leaders I have ever known. And to my three children, Sam, Ashley, and Hannah—the best teachers I have ever had.

—BT

To Freeman, Connor, and Savannah, who've been faithful supporters of my yearning to write and complete this book. And to the many talented and inspirational leaders whom I've had the good fortune to coach over the years.

—HOJ

CONTENTS

INTRODUCTION

There are countless ways of defining leadership. Because this is a book for and about leaders, we offer our own definition. As you consider it, notice what part of this definition resonates most with you.

Leadership is the ability to call forth your own best efforts, and the best efforts of others, to achieve a shared future that people care about.

What does it take for you to "call forth your own best efforts" day in and day out? How do you simultaneously maximize your own potential and the potential of those you lead? Where can you find the time and energy you need to envision a new future—one that you truly care about and that is shared by others as well?

As leadership coaches with more than forty years of combined experience, we're uniquely positioned to guide you along this journey. In addition to executive coaching and team coaching, Heather has consulted for more than eighteen years in the fields of organization development and conflict resolution, helping clients reignite their shared purpose, overcome differences, and work toward common goals. A Certified Somatic Coach with more than twenty-five years of coaching and leadership development experience, Bridgette specializes in coaching senior and emerging leaders in organizations facing rapid growth and change. We've partnered on this book to bring you the benefit of our experience working with leaders just like you who are ready to maximize their potential, revitalize their commitments, and lead their teams and organizations to new levels of success. Like you, our clients are committed not just to being great leaders but also to building great teams. *Missing Conversations* isn't just a book—it's a road map to your future.

We've worked with hundreds of leaders over the past twenty-five years, and we've learned that conversations are a leader's most influential tool for creating a shared future that people care about. Our first glimpse into the power that conversations have to shape how we see ourselves, and how we see others, happened many years ago, in an unlikely place—a first-grade classroom.

A six-year-old girl sits at a table facing her teacher. While her mother holds her hand under the table for moral support, the young girl quietly tells her teacher that she is often scared in the classroom. The reason for her fear? The teacher's habit of yelling at the first graders and sometimes even slamming her fist on their desks in frustration.

"When you do that, it makes me really scared," the young student says, "and it makes it hard for me to learn." Though her voice is soft, her words are strong. Her teacher, caught off-guard and humbled by her student's honesty and courage, vows to stop yelling and promises to do better at managing her frustration in the classroom—and she keeps her word.

But even more significant than the teacher's actions is the impact the conversation has on the little girl, who leaves the conversation standing a bit taller, walking more lightly, and feeling more secure.

Conversations like this one, which we helped one of our daughters have many years ago, don't get any easier the older we get. As we've discovered in our work with leaders, there are numerous "Missing Conversations" in organizations—conversations that people delay having or neglect altogether because they are uncomfortable, don't know how to engage in them, or don't even realize these conversations are missing.

Our understanding of conversations and the vital role they play in a leader's success continued to evolve when we attended a program for executive coaches taught by one of our mentors, Bob Dunham.[1] When Bob brought up the concept of "Missing Conversations"—the conversations leaders should be having with their direct reports, teams, and peers—it was a lightbulb moment for us. We began to listen intentionally for the conversations that our clients weren't having and helped them spot these conversations rather than overlook them. We coached our clients to face and enter into these conversations in more skillful and effective ways. Doing so had a profound impact on their leadership and on the results they were able to achieve.

We also began listening for another type of conversation that was often missing in our clients' lives—the conversations they needed to have, first and foremost, with themselves. It turns out that these were every bit as important to our clients' success as the more "outward-facing" conversations and were often their impetus for seeking coaching in the first place. As we helped our clients to turn the spotlight of their attention inward and engage in these conversations, our clients became clearer and more grounded in who they were, what they really cared about, and how they could best manage themselves in the midst of the chaos and uncertainty surrounding them. As a result of this inner journey, they began to show up in their leadership roles with greater clarity, conviction, and resolve.

We've discovered that nine simple but powerful questions compel leaders to engage in these critical internal conversations. While other leadership books focus on improving the quality of interpersonal conversations, this is the first book that explicitly names the nine conversations leaders must have with themselves. Over the course of our work with clients in hundreds of organizations both large and small, these conversations emerged as the most essential to a leader's positive impact and effectiveness. Each chapter of this book poses a key question and focuses you on one of these nine conversations, while providing you with a framework for engagement. We'll support you in deepening your self-awareness, boosting your satisfaction in the workplace, and accelerating your professional and personal success—and we'll show you how to motivate those you lead to do the same.

Dee Hock, founder and CEO Emeritus of Visa, made the case for ongoing reflection and development when he said, "If you seek to lead, invest at least fifty percent of your time in leading yourself—your own purpose, ethics, principles, motivation, and conduct." After all, if you can't lead and inspire yourself, how can you expect to lead and inspire others?

Overview

This book is organized into three parts. Part I introduces you to three conversations that will deepen your self-awareness, an essential ingredient of effective leadership. These conversations will provide you with a framework for exploring your identity as a leader, your impact on others, and your responses to the people and situations that trigger you. The net result? Greater authenticity and credibility as a leader, along with more equanimity in your day.

Part II presents three conversations that are inextricably linked to your own professional satisfaction and fulfillment. You'll explore how to better manage your capacity, discover proven practices for strengthening your well-being, and examine how best to navigate the inevitable career crossroads you will face. Having engaged in these conversations, you'll be better equipped to sustain your leadership efforts over time and to take care of yourself in the process. You'll also have the tools you need to chart a clear future path—whether that's with your current organization or in a radical new direction.

Part III covers three conversations focused on accelerating your success. You'll have an opportunity to get reacquainted with what inspires you and to envision a new future that you and others care about. We'll guide you to bring your best thinking and focused attention to the priorities and projects that matter most. And you'll assess the quality of your connections with the people you supervise, report to, and work alongside of. Most importantly, you'll learn what you can do to repair and rebuild trust where needed.

HOW TO USE THIS BOOK

At the heart of this book are stories of actual leaders with whom we've worked. Each story is followed with a "Your Turn" section that invites you to pause and engage more deeply with the material you are reading. We encourage you to take the time to do this exercise. Have a notebook and pen ready beside you so you can capture your responses to our questions and document your results to our exercises. Reading this book is more than a search for more knowledge: it's an actual experience that deepens your wisdom, enhances your skillful action, and enriches your presence.

Our Missing Conversations Self-Assessment (see page xix) is a tool we've created to support you as you move through this book. This Self-Assessment highlights your current strengths and where you can continue to grow and will direct you to the conversations that will benefit you the most. The book can be read sequentially, but each chapter stands on its own, allowing you to prioritize the areas you need to focus on most.

If you want to develop your potential, insight alone is not enough; you must also take new action and cultivate new habits. Toward this end, we have included a list of recommended action steps and supporting practices at the end of each chapter. We've also included supplemental tools in the appendix. These resources will help you take your leadership journey around a particular conversation to an even deeper level.

This book was written first and foremost for leaders to help them access more of their innate potential. It was also written for the coaches who work with them. If you are a coach, the conversations in this book provide a rigorous and thorough curriculum for a nine-month coaching engagement, with a chapter or conversation to focus on each month. You can also have your clients take the Missing Conversations Self-Assessment and, on the basis of their results, customize how much or how many of the conversations you include as part of your work with them.

Final Thoughts

We've worked with hundreds of leaders in major organizations over the course of our careers, and we know leadership is not for the faint of heart—in fact, we think the only thing more difficult than being a great leader is being a great parent!

We also know how challenging it is to lead well in the digital era, when our lives are beset by twenty-four-hour connectivity, constant uncertainty, and challenges our ancestors couldn't have even imagined. Now more than ever, leaders must be skilled in maximizing their own potential and helping those they lead to do the same.

We dedicate this book to all the leaders with whom we have had the privilege of working; many of their stories are told in these pages. We also dedicate this book to you, the reader. Our deepest wish is that you will find the hope, inspiration, and insights you need to keep your leadership flame alive and burning brightly. More than ever, the world needs leaders like you—those who are willing to do the deeper work of transforming themselves and, in doing so, transform their world.

MISSING CONVERSATIONS SELF-ASSESSMENT

Directions: Take a few minutes to complete the following assessment by placing a check mark next to each statement that is consistently true for you. When you are done, use the Interpretation Key to determine which Missing Conversations are most urgent for you.

Identity Conversation

- ☐ I'm comfortable in my own skin as a leader.
- ☐ I can clearly articulate and leverage my unique leadership strengths.
- ☐ I can name my leadership values and routinely communicate them in a clear and compelling way.

Impact Conversation

- ☐ I'm clear and confident about the impact I want to have on others.
- ☐ I regularly observe the impact of my moods, posture, and verbal communication and adjust them accordingly.
- ☐ I actively solicit feedback about how I'm doing from the people with whom I work.

Triggers Conversation

- ☐ I know what kind of people, events, and circumstances trigger me.
- ☐ When triggered, I am able to pause and regain my center before taking action.
- ☐ People tell me that I'm a calm and grounded presence—even in stressful situations.

CAPACITY CONVERSATION

- ☐ I am consistently able to deliver on my commitments without burning myself (or others) out.
- ☐ I am skillful at pushing back on unreasonable requests and in negotiating counteroffers.
- ☐ I know where the line is between taking on enough work and taking on too much, both for me and for my organization.

WELL-BEING CONVERSATION

- ☐ I wake up most mornings feeling refreshed and eager to start my day.
- ☐ I take periodic breaks from my work to rest and refuel.
- ☐ I regularly assess my well-being and make adjustments accordingly.

CAREER CROSSROADS CONVERSATION

- ☐ I am clear about what constitutes my ideal work.
- ☐ I feel at peace about the career path I am currently following.
- ☐ I look forward to starting my workweek.

INSPIRATION CONVERSATION

- ☐ I am optimistic about the future for my team and/or organization.
- ☐ I stay connected to those activities at work that inspire and enliven me.
- ☐ I engage others in shaping and creating the future.

STRATEGIC FOCUS CONVERSATION

- ☐ I am clear on my top priorities at work.
- ☐ I bring my best thinking and my focused attention to the projects and priorities that matter most.
- ☐ I consistently make room in my schedule for reflection, strategizing, dreaming, and planning.

Relationship Conversation

- ☐ My most important relationships at work reflect high levels of trust and open, direct communication.
- ☐ I actively engage in sincere efforts to rebuild trust in my relationships when I notice a breakdown.
- ☐ People find me open and fully present when they interact with me.

Interpretation Key

1. Which conversations above have no check marks, or only one? These are your Missing Conversations, and their absence is most likely undermining your self-awareness, satisfaction, and/or success. We recommend that you start with these chapters or pay special attention to them as you read through the book.

2. Which conversations have only two check marks? Though they are not entirely missing from your leadership repertoire, these conversations are most likely incomplete. We recommend you read these chapters with an eye for discovering which elements of these conversations need more of your careful attention.

3. Which conversations have three check marks? These represent areas of strength for you as a leader. Read these chapters to gain additional insight into what you do well as a leader and to find new tools for mentoring and coaching others.

PART I

Conversations That Deepen Self-Awareness

We cannot change what we are not aware of, and once we are aware, we cannot help but change.

—**Sheryl Sandberg,** *Lean In: Women, Work, and the Will to Lead*

Hans Christian Andersen's story "The Emperor's New Clothes" is a tale many of us were introduced to at a young age but can still recall years later. Why does this fable make such an impression? Is it because the image of a naked emperor parading through town is so outlandish that we can't help but remember it vividly? Or is there another, just as compelling reason that a story written in 1837 has such an enduring impact?

Andersen's tale touches a nerve because we can relate in some way to the emperor, a person who has become so removed from self-awareness that he's convinced himself that his "birthday suit" is a new set of dazzling clothes. As is often the case with those in leadership positions, no one around him has the courage to tell him the truth. There's something about his vulnerability that invites our empathy. We recognize that we, too, can lose sight of who we are and how others see us.

In the case of the emperor, his arrogance blocked his self-awareness. For many of the leaders we've worked with, it's not arrogance but activity that clouds their perception. The unrelenting pace of leadership leaves little time to pause, reflect, and self-examine.

Sound familiar?

If you're a busy leader who longs to become reacquainted with who you really are, this section was written for you. The three chapters included in this section will invite you to deepen your self-awareness through assessment, reflection, and action. Enhancing your self-awareness is the first step toward becoming more masterful in your leadership. After all, you can't identify changes you want to make or strengths you want to leverage differently if you aren't aware of them. As you become more familiar with who you are and how you impact others, you will lead from a place of greater authenticity. You'll also become more skillful at self-management, even when difficult circumstances test you. And you'll have a new lens through which to see yourself—along with new possibilities for action.

CHAPTER 1

Who Am I As a Leader? The Identity Conversation

Let the world know you as you are,
not as you think you should be,
because sooner or later, if you are posing,
you will forget the pose, and then where are you?

—**Fanny Brice**

If you've picked up this book, you're looking for answers. Whether you're new to leadership or a seasoned executive, it's likely you've been seeking wisdom on what it takes to lead effectively. If you're frequently scanning the countless titles of newly published books on leadership and filling your office with resources, you're not alone. Whether it's biographies of leaders or books that offer a new slant on how to influence or lead with conviction, you build your library hoping to learn something new about great leadership. Even if reading about leadership isn't a habit of yours, chances are you've been making and filing away a mental checklist of an effective leader's most important skills and attributes. You're in search of the secret formula—the proven path to leadership success.

This quest to discover what's behind the curtain of artful leadership is shared by most leaders and leadership coaches alike. We're convinced that with the right information and a hearty dose of self-discipline, we can improve our outcomes and inspire those we lead toward even greater results. It's a commonly held belief that we're not enough as we are, and we should be striving to be better.

But what if, in this quest to improve ourselves, we lose sight of who we really are?

In this chapter, we invite you to pause and reacquaint yourself with the core truth of who you are. You're already holding many of the answers you're looking for. No leadership theory or framework can substitute for the insights that live inside of you. Knowing yourself is fundamental to leading with confidence and clarity. You can't inspire others toward action if you are unsure and unsteady about what you stand for and what you have to offer.

Too many leaders we know get swallowed up in a tsunami of constant crises and lose touch with themselves. In the process of reacting to competing demands, they sacrifice the introspective time necessary to remain connected to their true selves. Some leaders with whom we work can no longer articulate why they chose to lead. Still others begin to wonder if they even belong in the ranks of leaders. They are victims of the "Impostor Syndrome"—secretly doubting their capacity to lead. And some leaders we coach find themselves mimicking other leaders rather than finding and trusting their unique leadership voice.

The Impostor Syndrome

The Impostor Syndrome is a surprisingly common experience for both emerging and seasoned leaders. This phenomenon doesn't discriminate; although female leaders report feeling fraudulent more often, it also affects men. Even the most successful leaders, as Facebook COO Sheryl Sandberg writes in her book *Lean In*, are susceptible to the siren song of self-doubt despite their many accomplishments.[1]

We have coached leaders in the most senior of positions who, while they may appear confident on the outside, secretly harbor doubts about their fit for leadership. They often feel as if they are missing a key ingredient that is essential to their success, such as charisma or deep industry knowledge—an ingredient that remains elusive despite their best efforts.

Leaders typically keep this self-doubt hidden from even their closest allies, family members, or friends for fear of being found out and seen as the fraud they believe themselves to be. This doubt is particularly common when a leader is promoted or hired into a challenging situation that he feels may be beyond his reach. The leader, vulnerable to self-doubt, becomes indecisive and cautious, which further erodes his self-confidence and undermines his ability to lead boldly.

In our experience, the Impostor Syndrome begins to dissolve when a leader learns that she is not alone in her feelings of self-doubt. Once she realizes she doesn't have to pretend to be someone else to succeed, she is able to trust in her innate strengths and skills.

How frequently are you caught up in confusion and self-doubt? If you're drawn to this chapter, you may be yearning to reconnect with your essential self. The Chinese philosopher Lao Tzu wrote, "He who knows others is learned; he who knows himself is enlightened."[2] How wise are you about yourself?

The 2006 comedy film *The Devil Wears Prada* reminds us that the journey toward self-discovery and wisdom can be filled with humor and insight. When Andy Sachs, the film's protagonist, takes a job in the intense, cutthroat world of high fashion, her world shifts dramatically. As an assistant to Miranda Priestly, editor in chief of a top fashion magazine, she discovers that the only way to succeed is to conform to her boss's exacting standards and contort herself to fit into the industry culture. In the process, Andy begins to lose sight of who she is and what she cares about. It's only when her life begins to unravel that she comes face-to-face with the costs of blending in and sacrificing her identity.

Andy recognizes that she's drifted too far from her core values and lost touch with her identity. By the end of the film, she regains her sense of self and chooses a new career path that better aligns with who she really is.

The Devil Wears Prada's message translates easily to leadership. Fulfillment only becomes possible when you live and lead authentically. But this journey toward self-discovery can be confusing. How do you find your unique leadership approach? Is it possible to meet the expectations of your organization without losing yourself in the process? What are your true gifts and talents, and how do you access them?

In this chapter, we invite you to simplify this journey and rediscover your own "brand" of leadership—one that calls forth who you are at your best and what you care about most. With increased self-awareness, you'll lead more effectively and from a place of greater authenticity and strength. Our three phases of reflection will encourage you to uncover assumptions that hold you back, name your true talents and gifts, and revisit your essential leadership values.

Phase 1: Uncover Your Beliefs and Assumptions

If you let your mind wander from this page and reflect back on the early leaders in your life who've made lasting impressions on you, who comes to mind? Was there a teacher whose leadership inspired you or a team coach who challenged you to play harder or run faster? Were your views of leadership shaped by a parent or a public figure you admired?

You may not often step back and consider the powerful influence that your early experiences have had on you. The stories you tell yourself about what it takes to be a successful leader live just below your consciousness and subtly inform your beliefs about who and how a leader needs to be. Your beliefs can often work in your favor and steer you in a positive direction—but they can also constrain you and undermine your potential. When you're convinced that you're missing some necessary skill or attribute and don't have what it takes to be a truly effective leader, you hold yourself back. You're less bold and courageous.

Do the beliefs and assumptions you hold about leadership enable you to thrive? Or do they hold you back?

When we ask leaders with whom we work to identify their long-held beliefs about effective leadership, they often respond with statements like, "Leaders have all the answers" and "Leaders are fearless." When spoken aloud, these assumptions suddenly ring false. Examining your beliefs in the light of day is the first step in testing them for their validity. In the process, you may discover that what you've been treating as true about leadership doesn't actually serve you.

Shaking Off Self-Doubt: Jessica's Story

A trained attorney, Jessica had served as a program director in her nonprofit organization until she assumed the executive director role when her predecessor retired. With her winning and warm smile, polished good looks, and energetic presence, she conveyed confidence in herself and her leadership.

Jessica had reached out for coaching because, despite her outwardly assured demeanor, she felt anxious in her new role. Often unable to sleep at night and pursued doggedly by thoughts of failure, she worried that she didn't have the "goods" to be effective in her new role. She complained of constant worries about potentially missed deadlines or forgotten priorities. She found it difficult to relax into her role and find satisfaction in her leadership.

Jessica had followed in the footsteps of a highly competent executive director, a woman who assumed many management and leadership responsibilities and who embodied a directive management approach. Her command-and-control style translated to long hours. She frequently involved herself in the minutiae of her staff's activities.

When we first sat down with Jessica, we could tell right away that she felt conflicted. She didn't want to model her own management approach after her predecessor's. Yet, she struggled with a belief that if she wasn't involved in every aspect of her organization's operations and an authority in every area, as her predecessor had been, she was somehow "less than" and ineffective. Her belief that she didn't possess the required level of expertise in every aspect of her role eroded her self-confidence. In striving toward perfection and unquestionable expertise, she experienced profound exhaustion.

Jessica's beliefs about herself and leadership had lodged her between a rock and a hard place. If she was true to her beliefs and assumptions about who she *should* be as a leader, she ended up feeling disconnected and fraudulent. If she held true to her beliefs about who she felt she really *was* as a leader, she saw herself as not up to the leadership challenge.

In our coaching sessions, Jessica actively challenged and decided to let go of the assumption that she needed to be an expert to lead, a shift that settled her anxiety and gave her the freedom to be imperfect. Her new belief that "leaders empower others" opened up possibilities for action. Unlike the executive director she'd replaced, who'd taken responsibility for a majority of key initiatives, she realized she could delegate important responsibilities to her team members. She began to recruit and count on experienced and talented volunteers to plan for a new, major fund-raising event rather than shouldering the burden entirely on her own. The "noise" in her head subsided as she began to trust herself in her leadership and clarify the role she believed she could play well. Ironically, the more she accepted a belief that she didn't need to be an expert to lead, the more confident and competent she actually became.

Your Turn

Having read Jessica's story, pause for a minute to examine your own leadership beliefs and assumptions. Use the inserted checklist on the next page to identify them, then reflect on the following questions:

1. What are your core beliefs about what it takes to be a great leader?
2. Like Jessica, most leaders have one core belief that is at the root of their self-doubt or dissatisfaction. Is this true for you? If so, what is it? How might this belief hold you back?

As you sit with these questions, you're likely to come up with some obvious and immediate answers. Dig a little deeper, though. To what extent do your assumptions about leadership either help or hinder you in your current role? Challenge yourself to move past the obvious and uncover the influences and messages that have shaped the view you hold of yourself as a leader today. Your unexamined and untested beliefs and assumptions are like invisible handcuffs that imprison you in self-limiting thinking and self-defeating behaviors.

At this stage of your reflection, what's become clearer for you about your beliefs and assumptions about leadership? Are there stories you've treated as true about you and what it takes to lead that may be getting in your way?

When you challenge your beliefs and assumptions, you step into a new level of engagement. This phase of your Identity Conversation reenrolls you in your leadership. As you question those buried beliefs that have influenced you, you reopen yourself to your leadership calling. You're no longer attached to a smaller version of yourself. You're free to remember what called you to assume a leadership role in the first place.

COMMON ASSUMPTIONS AND BELIEFS ABOUT LEADERS CHECKLIST

Review the following list and check off the assumptions with which you agree:

- ☐ Great leaders are charismatic.
- ☐ Leaders are natural visionaries.
- ☐ Leaders are gifted communicators.
- ☐ Leaders are born, not made.
- ☐ Effective leaders only make decisions through consensus.
- ☐ Leaders should have all the answers.
- ☐ Leaders are bold and fearless.
- ☐ The best leaders are outgoing and extroverted.
- ☐ Effective leaders are popular and well liked.
- ☐ Strong leaders don't show vulnerability.
- ☐ A leader should always be in control.
- ☐ Leaders have powerful, commanding personalities.
- ☐ The best leaders are subject matter experts.
- ☐ Great leaders never fail.
- ☐ A powerful leader is highly competent in every function of the organization.
- ☐ The best leaders work longer and harder than anyone else to achieve results.

Now you're positioned to step back and ask yourself, "What is my compelling reason to lead?" Remind yourself why you said yes to leadership. If you acknowledge the events and circumstances that have led you to precisely where you are in your career right now, what do you see? As you face the future, what purpose are you fulfilling by continuing on the leadership pathway?

Once you've acknowledged and released yourself from ungrounded beliefs and reenrolled yourself in your commitment to lead, you're better positioned to identify and capitalize on your strengths. The burden of self-doubt lightens, and you're freer to claim and leverage those gifts that will help you realize your potential.

Phase 2: Claim Your True Talents and Gifts

Some leaders with whom we work live in a persistent state of quietly questioning their abilities. Like the nightly news broadcast that highlights trouble spots in our world, they focus their attention on what's broken in their leadership and what's missing in their skills set. They're not alone. Many leaders tend to direct their attention toward their deficiencies and, with laser-like precision, hone in on their inadequacies. Trapped in this perspective of deficiency, they find themselves stuck in a cycle of self-doubt, cautious about the leadership moves they make and reluctant to take risks.

If we were to ask you to assess your leadership, what grade would you give yourself? Are you looking first at your deficiencies or your abilities? If you're like many of the leaders we work with, you're likely to focus your attention on your development needs. It's not an unusual tendency. In fact, as *Buddha's Brain* author Dr. Rick Hanson suggests, the human brain is actually hardwired to operate like Velcro for negative experiences and thoughts and like Teflon for positive ones.[3] Why? Without the ability to assess threats around them, our early ancestors never would have survived a dangerous world.

So what's the trouble with this approach? While most of us no longer live in a life-or-death environment, our biology hasn't quite caught up with our current reality. We tend to function as if we're still living in the bush and on alert for predators—and our energy follows our attention. If we habitually focus almost exclusively on what we need to fix about ourselves, our deficiencies grow in importance, and we begin to overlook our strengths.

Placing too much of your focus on deficiencies—whether others' or your own—is a habit that undermines optimism and ambition, two qualities that are associated with effective leadership. When you step back and consider the leaders you most admire, do they play to their strengths or focus on their deficiencies? Your role models most likely orient their leadership toward their strengths. Not surprisingly, a strengths-based perspective generates a more positive and resourceful mood in organizations. As you read about the Impact Conversation in chapter 2, you'll take a closer look at the topic of mood and assess your own prevailing mood and its impact. For now, consider how much more creative and productive you are when you assess your leadership with *equal* attention to your strengths and development needs.

If you put as much energy into claiming and cultivating your strengths as you do into addressing your development needs, who might you become?

Regaining Strength: Ben's Story

Ben had a proven track record of leading teams and generating great results in a highly charged, intense hospital environment. With a broad and infectious smile and laugh, he had a way of putting people at ease quickly. But despite his reputation, when Ben came to us for guidance, he was under great stress. His boss, the hospital's CFO, focused exclusively on Ben's shortcomings. Ben, who had received glowing performance reviews and feedback from his previous boss, was initially perplexed. His confusion turned to discomfort and, eventually, to anxiety.

Ben was viewed hospital-wide as a problem solver and a motivating and inspirational leader. Before his troubled relationship with his boss, he was a leader others turned to for support and guidance. By the time we started coaching Ben, he'd begun to question his capacity to lead. His self-confidence, once high, had taken a severe hit. As a result, he'd begun to question his every leadership move and second-guess his strengths. His deepening anxiety about how his boss viewed him dominated his thoughts and clouded his perspective. Absorbed exclusively in his perceived shortcomings, his energy for his leadership role waned.

It was immediately clear to us that Ben needed to give his self-doubt a swift kick in the rear and reclaim his strengths and true talents. Before he could focus on dealing with his hypercritical boss, he needed to remind himself of his past successes and acknowledge the strengths that had enabled him to achieve these wins.

Within several coaching sessions that focused Ben primarily on surfacing and recognizing his strengths, he had regained his sense of self. He rediscovered and acknowledged his talent for building relationships and developing a highly committed team. He reclaimed his gifts of dedication and determination. In short, he gave himself credit for those innate abilities that had served him well in his career.

His self-confidence restored, Ben was able to skillfully confront his boss about their communication issues and working relationship. Ultimately, he recognized that he could no longer work successfully with his boss and initiated a career move. Ben chose a new position in a different hospital and transitioned to a setting where he could lead confidently from his strengths.

Your Turn

It's your turn to dive into this element of the Identity Conversation. Take a few minutes to complete the inserted Strong Leader Checklist. Then consider the follow questions in light of your results:

1. What leadership strengths come to you most naturally and easily?
2. When you are using these strengths, what kind of an impact are you able to have on the people and the organization you lead?
3. Is there a particular strength you have as a leader that you tend to devalue or dismiss? If so, what might be possible if you owned this strength and fully embraced it as a valuable asset that you bring to the table?

THE STRONG LEADER CHECKLIST

Directions: Effective leadership requires that we know our strengths and how to leverage them fully for the benefit of others. Take a few minutes to review the following list and check off anything that fits who you are and how you lead. *Which statements describe your particular gifts and strengths?*

- ☐ I see into the future. I constantly think about where my organization is going and how to get there. (c)
- ☐ I am a good communicator. I articulate my messages in a clear and compelling way. (a)
- ☐ I know how to remove the obstacles that keep my people from playing at their best. (e)
- ☐ I see the untapped potential in others. (b)
- ☐ I'm organized and have systems in place that keep me focused. (c)
- ☐ When chaos is swirling all around, I am able to keep my wits about me and provide calm, clear direction to others. (d)
- ☐ When presented with a challenge or problem, my mind immediately generates possible solutions, and I can quickly spot the best way forward. (c)
- ☐ I hold employees accountable for the commitments they make. If they fail to deliver as promised, I know how to confront them firmly yet fairly. (d)
- ☐ I'm known for having a great sense of humor. I value laughter and having fun with others. (a)
- ☐ I'm skillful at maneuvering my way around obstacles and challenges. (c)
- ☐ I am a good mentor. People grow and develop around me. (b)

- ☐ I know how to work the system to get things accomplished in a timely manner. (e)
- ☐ I excel at execution. Things get done well and on time when I'm involved. (e)
- ☐ I don't shy away from conflict and confrontation. In fact, I am good at facing and addressing them head-on. (d)
- ☐ I am an effective networker. I build strong connections both inside and outside my organization. (a)
- ☐ I am a keen observer of what makes others tick, and I know how to motivate them accordingly. (b)
- ☐ I am a straight shooter. Others always know where I stand on issues. (d)
- ☐ I pick up on and empathize easily with the cares and concerns of others. (a)
- ☐ I am a good team builder. I know how to take a group with different personalities and skill sets and build them into a cohesive team with a shared purpose. (b)
- ☐ I put people at ease and can connect with just about anyone. (a)
- ☐ I'm a great planner. Things rarely fall through the cracks when I'm around. (e)
- ☐ I give people lots of feedback, both positive and constructive. (b)
- ☐ I'm great with numbers and know how to use them to make a strong business case for the initiatives I lead. (e)
- ☐ I stand strong in my character and values. As a result, most people trust and believe in me. (d)
- ☐ I have a talent for connecting the dots between ideas and/or situations. (c)
- ☐ I am a great coach. I enjoy helping the people around me discover their own solutions to the problems and challenges they face. (b)

- ☐ I find it easy to win others over, even strangers. (a)
- ☐ I am decisive. I make decisions thoughtfully and expeditiously. (d)
- ☐ I keep myself and others focused on a few critical priorities rather than getting lost in the trivial many. (c)
- ☐ I am politically savvy and know how to get things done by developing the right relationships. (e)

Scoring key: Add up your answers for each letter. The higher your score for a particular letter, the more your strengths are concentrated in that category. If your answers are high in a number of categories, you have a broad palette of strengths from which to draw.

Mostly "a" answers: Your strengths are related to **Building Rapport and Connection**

Mostly "b" answers: Your strengths are related to **Developing People and Teams**

Mostly "c" answers: Your strengths are related to **Thinking and Acting Strategically**

Mostly "d" answers: Your strengths are related to **Leading with Clarity, Accountability, and Calm**

Mostly "e" answers: Your strengths are related to **Executing and Getting Things Done**

How comfortable are you naming and claiming your strengths? What does your comfort level tell you about your ability to fully own your talents? The greater your discomfort with noticing and acknowledging your strengths, the greater likelihood that you're not utilizing them fully in your leadership. Focusing your attention on your strengths isn't a Pollyanna move designed to nourish your ego. Rather, it's a deliberate and calculated strategy we encourage you to pursue so you can experience the benefits of acknowledging what you do well.

One benefit you'll enjoy is a renewed confidence in your leadership among those you lead. Intentionally focusing on your talents and gifts will also generate an energetic shift that opens you up to new possibilities for action. You'll renew your belief in your capacity to succeed. In her book *Positivity,* positive psychology researcher Dr. Barbara Frederickson documents the tested and proven correlation between positivity and new possibilities. What many of us have intuitively known to be true about the relationship between a positive outlook and greater success and satisfaction in our lives and careers has now been studied and laboratory tested. Frederickson suggests that positivity opens up our hearts and our minds, positioning us to become more receptive and creative as a result.[4]

What better application of these research findings on the power of a positive focus than for you to pause and acknowledge your innate strengths and talents? And while we encourage you to give attention to your strengths, we're not suggesting that you overlook gaps in your skills that hold you back or tendencies that undermine your leadership. Leading authentically also requires that you recognize and own your weaknesses and acknowledge when you're overusing your strengths in a way that may actually jeopardize your success. To be true to yourself, you need to seek out your shadow side as well as celebrate your strengths and potential.

We'll talk more about exploring your shadow side in chapter 2. For now, keep your attention firmly focused on your strengths and what you do well. A holistic approach to seeing yourself is crucial to living and leading authentically. Our clients have taught us that exploring and naming their strengths is an all-too-unfamiliar experience. Once introduced, it's a practice that brings balance and perspective to how they view themselves.

Once you are more aware of your beliefs and assumptions about leadership and yourself and acknowledge your gifts and talents, you're poised to examine your guiding principles—the core values that serve as your leadership compass. As you move into the next phase of the Identity Conversation, you'll make your values explicit and recommit to what's important to you.

PHASE 3: ACKNOWLEDGE WHAT YOU CARE ABOUT MOST

How often do you stop and reflect on what matters most to you? Do you routinely pause to consider whether your actions and decisions align with what you care about most?

It's easy to misplace or even lose your sense of what's meaningful in our hyperconnected, twenty-four-hour culture. Your energy and attention are pulled toward your most immediate circumstances and concerns. You may find yourself trapped in a cycle of activity that's often out of step with your true interests and values.

Values are those personal principles that live inside you. Unlike morals, which are shaped by the society we live in, they reflect your own unique imprint and are coded to your individual needs and interests. The more you honor them in your life, the deeper satisfaction you'll experience personally and professionally.

When leaders lose touch with the guiding principles they most want to embody, they compromise their integrity and put their organization's reputation—as well as their own—on the line. Sadly, we don't have to look too far to find stories about leaders who espouse certain leadership values but demonstrate otherwise through their actions and decisions. In the process, they sabotage their careers, land front-page stories in national newspapers, and jeopardize their organization's well-being.

Engaging in a conversation about your core leadership values can be unchartered territory. Think about your own situation. When was the last time you stepped back and assessed whether the actions you're taking are actually in sync with what you value most as a leader? Do your choices reflect what you truly care about? When you last made a critical leadership decision, were your core values, or leadership principles, guiding you?

Steve Jobs, of Apple fame, introduced an innovative approach for overcoming the challenge of naming core values when he launched an ad campaign designed to remind consumers and employees alike of the values central to Apple's identity.

In Walter Isaacson's biography of Steve Jobs, Jobs describes the ad campaign that Apple launched when he became CEO during his second stint with the company. "Think Different" was the motto, and it appeared at the bottom of a series of photos of iconic people like Albert Einstein, Amelia Earhart, and Thomas Edison.

Jobs said that the ad campaign was directed not only at customers but also at employees. "We at Apple had forgotten who we were," he explained. "One way to remember who you are is to remember who your heroes are."[5]

When you reawaken the connection between the leader you are and the values you cherish, you infuse your actions, decisions, and conversations with greater purpose and clarity. You telegraph your integrity to your team and customers. You become more credible in your leadership when people around you understand what you stand for. Our client Tom's story illustrates what's possible when you align your values with your leadership.

Rediscovering True North: Tom's Story

Tom was the founder and CEO of a fast-growing Internet company. He was known for his keen intellect, his business development savvy, and his skills as a strategic thinker. He loved his business, particularly the outward-facing aspects of his role, and enjoyed wooing clients and finding new markets for his company's services.

Though Tom loved his work, he felt frustrated with his management team. The team was not communicating effectively, and their meetings could be painfully long and unproductive. Tom came to us for help with what he saw as a team problem—and soon realized that the real issue was his leadership.

In our first couple of coaching sessions, we asked Tom about his values and guiding principles. Tom identified himself as a collaborative decision maker and stressed the importance of reaching decisions through consensus. He also brought up integrity, honesty, and loyalty. Tom told us he thought leaders should be brave, fearless, and charismatic. Yet the more he talked, the less convinced we became that Tom clearly knew what he stood for. Although he had unmistakable ideas about how a leader *should* behave, what seemed less clear to us was whether Tom knew who *he* was as a leader. What did he really value?

Tom asked us to attend several of his management team meetings and give him feedback on how to improve them. When we observed these meetings, several things became clear to us about the team's decision-making process and Tom's role in shaping it. Though he asked for input and sought consensus, Tom's body language contradicted his words. Instead of being open and engaging in these moments, he appeared tense and closed off. We also noticed that the team frequently got bogged down in these discussions. Several times they were unable to agree on a decision—or even identify what decision they needed to make.

When we met with Tom for our next coaching session, we shared our assessment with him about his body language. Tom admitted he was conflicted: "I suppose I think I *should* make decisions collaboratively and that I *should* value consensus, but if I'm being truly honest with myself, I don't," he said. When we gave Tom permission to speak honestly about what he truly valued, he was able to identify four values that really mattered to him: loyalty, innovation, adaptability, and teamwork. He was passionate about these values and could articulate why they mattered not only to him but also to the success of the company. It turned out that consensus and collaborative decision-making didn't make the list. It wasn't that Tom didn't value his team's input, because he did. But the truth was, he didn't believe many decisions could or should be made by consensus, and he didn't think it was wise to run his company that way.

While Tom had tried to live up to his team's expectations and to lead as if he valued consensus, his management team had begun to suspect otherwise. They could sense when Tom had already made up his mind on key decisions and was just going through the motions of asking for their input.

This misalignment between what Tom *said* he valued and how he actually led was beginning to erode their trust. It was also sapping Tom's energy.

Tom realized that he needed to align his leadership behavior with his values. As a step in this direction, we suggested he share his core values with his management team and talk about why these were important to him. He did, and he also invited his team members to share their values with each other. In the process, Tom's team discovered that some of their individual values were the same. These shared values became an important part of their team "norms" and also served as touch points they could turn to when they faced important decisions.

Tom made a point to be more transparent with his team about decision-making. When he had already made up his mind, he let them know, and when he truly needed their input, he asked for it and acted upon it. Over time, the management team meetings became not only more transparent but more productive as well. As Tom led more consistently and transparently from his true values, he reclaimed his integrity. He also discovered his authentic leadership voice.

Your Turn

How clear are you about your core leadership values? We invite you to use the inserted Leadership Values Checklist to identify those that are essential to your leadership. Once you've identified your top ten, use the following questions to gain more clarity:

1. What are your three to five most important values? Why are these important to you as a leader?

2. In the last six months, how aligned have your leadership actions, choices, and focus been with your top three to five values?

3. How much harmony is there between your values and your leadership?

TOP TEN LEADERSHIP VALUES

From the following list, check off the ten values that resonate most with you. Check only those values you honestly feel are integral to your work and to your role as a leader. Feel free to add any values that don't appear on our list but that you consider essential.

- ☐ Adaptability
- ☐ Autonomy
- ☐ Boldness
- ☐ Challenge
- ☐ Collaboration
- ☐ Commitment
- ☐ Compassion
- ☐ Competition
- ☐ Connection
- ☐ Creativity
- ☐ Curiosity
- ☐ Determination
- ☐ Diligence
- ☐ Discipline
- ☐ Excellence
- ☐ Fairness
- ☐ Flexibility
- ☐ Fun
- ☐ Growth
- ☐ Harmony
- ☐ Honesty
- ☐ Innovation
- ☐ Inspiration
- ☐ Joy
- ☐ Kindness
- ☐ Loyalty
- ☐ Mastery
- ☐ Partnership
- ☐ Passion
- ☐ Pride
- ☐ Productivity
- ☐ Purpose
- ☐ Reliability
- ☐ Resilience
- ☐ Resolve
- ☐ Resourcefulness
- ☐ Respect
- ☐ Risk Taking
- ☐ Security
- ☐ Stability
- ☐ Teamwork
- ☐ Tradition
- ☐ Transparency
- ☐ Trust
- ☐ Wisdom
- ☐ Others:

When you declare your allegiance to your leadership values and give them your conscious attention, you remember your essential self. But under stress, we often make choices that distance us from what matters most to us. We slip into a pattern of sacrificing our core leadership values. Extricating ourselves from this pattern becomes an enormous challenge, often because we've convinced ourselves that this way of leading is our only option.

As poet and author David Whyte notes in his book *The Heart Aroused,* "one of the disciplines of building a rich soul life seems to be the simple act, on a daily basis, of remembering what is most important to us."[6] Your soulful satisfaction increases as you remind yourself what is most important to you. Leading in a way that is congruent with your core values ensures your integrity as a leader. People follow a leader who is clear and grounded in what she stands for.

By engaging in this element of the Identity Conversation, you are rigorously examining the gap between how you are leading today and what matters most to you. Awareness of this gap can reshape the choices you make and the actions you take.

The Identity Conversation: Key Takeaways

Ralph Waldo Emerson once said, "To be yourself in a world that is constantly trying to make you something else is the greatest accomplishment." By engaging in the Identity Conversation, you've rediscovered the best of who you really are as a leader and let go of who you or others think you ought to be. You've unearthed the beliefs and assumptions that held you back in the past. You've taken a fresh look at your true talents and gifts—the strengths that are essential to your own unique brand of leadership. By giving yourself the space and opportunity to reconnect with what you care about and value most in your leadership and life, you've opened up a space for greater alignment and joy. Having engaged in your own Identity Conversation, you're now poised to lead from a place of greater authenticity and strength.

The Identity Conversation: What's Next?

Coaching Assignments for Leveraging Your Learning

Is the Identity Conversation particularly critical for you? The following list of Actions, Practices, and Resources is a tool kit for engaging more deeply in this important Missing Conversation.

Action Steps

- Distribute the Strong Leader Checklist to your boss, peers, and direct reports to solicit their input on your leadership strengths and talents.
- Ask five people you trust to share stories of you at your best in your leadership. Listen closely to their stories and note which of your strengths and skills these stories highlight.
- As you grapple with the question of who you are as a leader and the values that live in your core, it can be helpful for you to reflect on who your heroes and heroines are. Our heroes often stand for the values that we come closest to embodying when we are most authentic and at our best. Identify your top three heroes/heroines and the values for which they stand.

Ongoing Practices

- For at least two weeks, at the end of each workday, capture your most significant "win" for the day and note what strength/s enabled you to achieve this win.
- Write down your top three leadership values and put them in a place that's visible to you. Touch base with this list when you have tough decisions to make or need to take action in a way that will be challenging for you or others.
- Make a point to regularly observe your inner dialogue about your worth and value as a leader. Notice if or when it spirals downward or when your attention becomes overly focused on your deficiencies. Course correct as needed.

Suggested Resources

Becoming a Resonant Leader: Develop Your Emotional Intelligence, Renew Your Relationships, Sustain Your Effectiveness by Annie McKee, Richard Boyatzis, and Frances Johnston: Harvard Business Press, 2008.

Leadership from the Inside Out: Becoming a Leader for Life by Kevin Cashman: Berrett-Koehler, 2008.

Strengths Finder 2.0 by Tom Rath: Gallup Press, 2007.

CHAPTER 2

How Do Others See Me? The Impact Conversation

Human beings almost always suffer from the disconnect between the self that we think we are and the self that others see in us.

—**Marshall Goldsmith,**
What Got You Here Won't Get You There

When Tiger Woods was at the zenith of his career, he was asked why he still worked with a coach. Given that he had achieved greatness as a professional golfer, the reporter wondered why he, of all people, needed one. Tiger's response was simple yet profound: "Because I can't see my own swing."

The truth is that it's difficult for any of us to "see our own swing." The people around us often have a clearer and more accurate picture of how we are coming across to others than we do. This is especially true for leaders. The further you move up in your organization, the more insulated you're likely to become. Given your position and the authority that comes with it, people are less likely to be truthful with you and more likely to tell you what they think you want to hear. It's as if you're in a protected bubble, cut off from the honest assessments and truth telling of those you lead.

Pause for a moment to consider the people around you, including your direct reports, colleagues, and peers. How many of them can you count on to give you truly honest feedback about how you are showing up as a leader? Who has the courage to tell you the unvarnished truth? In our experience, most leaders are lucky if they have one such person.

Stepping outside of this leadership bubble takes courage. Inevitably, you'll uncover gaps between how you *want* to come across to others and how you actually *do.* The goal of the Impact Conversation is to close these gaps. As you do, your credibility and influence expand.

Before you can close these gaps, however, you must first acknowledge they exist. Until you do, you are essentially leading blind.

This was the case for three leaders you'll meet later in this chapter. Their blind spots around certain aspects of their leadership presence created obstacles both for them and for the people they led. As you read their stories, you'll have an opportunity to consider your own leadership blind spots. Perhaps you'll discover that certain aspects of your leadership style or presence make it difficult for people to do their best work. These negative blind spots, once seen and understood, can be a source of transformation, enabling you to lead in new and more inspiring ways.

As you learned in chapter 1, it's just as easy to overlook your strengths as it is to overlook your weaknesses. Through the Impact Conversation, you'll gain new insight into the positive difference you make in people's lives—ways you impact your colleagues, family members, and community for the better that you were previously unable to see. These positive blind spots, once seen and embraced, can be a source of inspiration for you and lead to renewed energy, effort, and engagement.

The three phases of the Impact Conversation will challenge you to explore how others see you and open up new possibilities for your leadership and growth. As you engage in the reflections that follow and act on the discoveries that come from them, your self-awareness, integrity, and credibility will grow. But the benefits extend even further. You'll also be shaping the *leadership culture* in your organization. Your participation in the Impact Conversation sets a powerful example for others to follow and creates new opportunities for your organization around giving and receiving honest feedback, fostering transparency, and creating trust.

Phase 1: Define the Impact You Want to Have

As a leader, your impact is profound and far-reaching—perhaps more so than you even realize. Everything you say and do is amplified and magnified by virtue of your position and authority. Your followers scrutinize you closely and are keenly attuned to and affected by your moods, your language, and your actions. Like a powerful ship, you create and leave a wake behind you.

This leadership wake expands as you move up in your organization, while the vacuum of feedback that surrounds you stays in place and even grows more impenetrable—unless you decide to do something about it. This is precisely why the Impact Conversation is so essential. Without it, you run the risk of wielding greater power while simultaneously becoming less aware of how this power is being seen and felt by those around you.

There are many studies revealing the impact leaders have on their organizations. Research shows, for example, that leaders strongly impact retention. The Gallup organization polled more than a million employees and found that a person's immediate manager is one of the top five predictors of employee turnover.[1]

For leaders, the question isn't whether you're having an impact, but rather, is it the one you want?

We've found that when leaders clearly and compellingly articulate the impact they want to have, they are inspired to make immediate positive shifts in their leadership. This was certainly the case for our client Sam.

Committing to Change: Sam's Story

Sam led a large accounting firm that was struggling to expand its business during a recent downturn in the economy. The path forward for his organization was filled with many obstacles. In Sam's eyes, his organization had become stagnant and complacent. He wanted to shift his company's culture so that it was characterized by greater ownership, innovation, and initiative.

Sam came to us because he didn't see these characteristics in many of his managers and employees. He complained about their lack of effort, their inconsistent commitment, and their lack of creativity. The more he focused on his employees' shortcomings, the more frustrated he became. Rather than focusing on his own functioning, Sam was fixated on what his employees weren't doing.

We challenged Sam to shift his focus from what his employees weren't doing to what *he* needed to do differently to lead his organization forward. What kind of leader did he aspire to be? What shifts might he need to make to engage his employees' best efforts?

The frustration and mounting pressures Sam was under had taken their toll, and under this strain, he'd resorted to behaviors he wasn't proud of. He admitted that he'd been highly critical of his employees, even raising his voice and berating people when they didn't measure up or couldn't give him the answers he wanted. Instead of being a challenging and inspiring leadership presence, he'd become a threatening one. Sam was stifling the very creativity and initiative that he wanted to see more of in his organization.

This was clearly *not* the impact he wanted to have, and to his credit, Sam faced this realization head-on.

We helped Sam craft an Impact Statement: a simple declaration articulating the kind of leader he aspired to be. Sam's Impact Statement was, "I am committed to leading others through *inspiration* rather than *intimidation,* and to helping those around me to reach their full potential." This declaration became a touchstone for Sam that he referred to on a daily basis. As a result, he began to make immediate changes in his leadership (we'll share more about *how* he did this in phase 3 of this chapter). Sam's renewed clarity and resolve were a key turning point in his leadership and, ultimately, in the life of his business.

Your Turn, Part 1: Reflection

The following questions are designed to help you think more deeply about the impact you want to have on those you lead. Take a few minutes to reflect upon your answers.

1. As poet Maya Angelou observed, "people will forget what you said, people will forget what you did, but people will never forget how you made them feel." How do you want people to feel in your presence: Heard? Valued? Committed? Optimistic? Inspired?

2. As we've mentioned previously, leaders always impact their people and their organizations for better or for worse. What impact do you want to have on the people you lead? How do you hope your employees and colleagues will be better off for having worked with you and for you?

3. What kind of an impact do you want to have on your organization? How do you want your company/division/team to be better off as a result of your leadership?

Your Turn, Part 2: Craft Your Own Impact Statement

Creating a clear, easy-to-remember statement of your leadership commitment is an essential element of the Impact Conversation. This commitment will become a touchstone for you and provide you with the clarity you need to take focused, intentional action. The following steps will help you craft your own Impact Statement.

Step 1: Take a look at the following sample Impact Statements from leaders we have worked with. Notice the similar structure that these statements follow and see what they may offer you in terms of stimulating your own thinking.

> "I am committed to being a results-oriented and compassionate leader who helps people reach their full potential."

> "I am committed to being a strategic leader who rises above daily distractions and keeps others focused on the big picture."

"I am committed to being a poised, nonanxious leader who exudes a calming effect on the projects and people I manage."

"I am committed to being a self-aware, adaptable leader who has found her own voice."

Step 2: Reflect on your answers to the questions in part 1 of this "*Your Turn*" section and use them to develop a draft of your own Impact Statement. Your Impact Statement should reflect your own leadership strengths and values and offer a challenge for future growth.

Use the structure we've provided if it helps:

"I am committed to being a ______________________________
leader, who ____."

Once you have a draft of your Impact Statement, read it out loud. What happens to your energy level? Do you feel inspired? Recharged? Recommitted?

Notice that your statement begins with the phrase, "I am *committed* to." This language is intentional. Your Impact Statement represents something deeper and more important than a wish or a desire: it is a commitment that you fully own and intend to fulfill.

On page 213 in the appendix, you'll find the Impact Statement and Actions Worksheet. This exercise will help your Impact Statement come alive in your leadership. A simple yet powerful practice is to read your Impact Statement aloud each morning before you launch into your busy day. This will remind you of the leader you are committed to being and the impact you want to have as you face the challenges and demands ahead.

PHASE 2: ASSESS THE IMPACT YOU HAVE

Armed with a clear and compelling Impact Statement, you're now ready to uncover any gaps that may exist between your intended impact and your actual one. None of us sets out to be a particular kind of leader and then *intentionally* behaves in ways that contradict our intentions. Yet at times, this is exactly what happens. Our client Jim learned this lesson the hard way.

Uncovering Blind Spots: Jim's Story

Jim's work as a senior project manager for an entrepreneurial company was filled with unrelenting pressure, unrealistic deadlines, and constant, last-minute changes. The stress of his job was starting to affect Jim's health and home life, so he reached out to us to see if we could help him to better manage it. He also wanted to learn how he could cultivate a more confident and poised leadership presence. Jim wanted to support his team by remaining calm and clear-headed in the midst of the chaos that surrounded them.

Several things struck us about Jim's presence when we met with him for a coaching session on a particularly busy and challenging day. The first thing we noticed was his speed. He walked at such a fast clip that we almost had to run to keep up with him as we headed down the hall to his office—and he spoke just as a fast as he walked. When he spoke, he appeared tense and anxious. His pace came across as frenetic rather than energetic. We could actually feel ourselves getting more anxious in his presence—no doubt the opposite result of his intended impact.

As we sat with Jim in his office, we asked his permission to share our observations and assessments, which he openly received. We described how he was coming across and the impact it was having on us. Using the metaphor of shifting gears in a car, we asked Jim what gear he felt he was operating in that day, and what gear he found himself in on most days. Was this speed and pace an anomaly or the status quo for him? Did he always operate in high gear, or could he downshift when needed?

Jim agreed to take on a practice of regularly observing the pace at which he moved through his day, particularly as he interacted with his staff. Each day he paused twice, at midmorning and midafternoon, took a conscious breath, and noticed the speed at which he was walking or talking. Was it appropriate for the situation at hand? How did his "gear" affect the people with whom he was interacting?

Jim also committed to start his day differently. He had a habit of rushing into work late and then simply diving into his day before he had even decided what was most important. Instead, he committed to taking a few minutes when he first arrived at the office to gather himself, review his priorities, and set a positive tone for the day.

Thanks to this work, Jim was able to make substantive course corrections. He was able to vary his speed according to the situation at hand and often "downshifted" when he was meeting with his team or mentoring an associate. This enabled him to better gauge his level of rapport and connection with others. Over time, Jim reported feeling calmer and more connected to his staff, and his employees noticed that he seemed more present and less anxious. The team's performance improved as well. Team members felt more comfortable sharing their ideas, and the lowered anxiety in the group enabled them to focus better, resulting in fewer mistakes and missed deadlines.

Your Turn

As a leader, you are constantly transmitting information and revealing yourself to others as you move through your day. Recall the Impact Statement that you crafted earlier. With this in mind, pause for a moment to consider the following questions:

1. To what extent is the way that you walk, talk, and interact with others consistent with your desired impact? In what ways might it not be?

2. Many leaders, like Jim, move at a pace that is fast and unrelenting. What pace are you keeping these days, and when and where might you "downshift"?

As Jim learned, to assess your impact on others, it's essential to gather feedback and develop your "observer muscle." These strategies help you step outside of the insulated bubble that we mentioned in the introduction to this chapter—the one that cuts you off from the assessments and honest truth telling of those you lead. Let's take a closer look at each of these methods. As we do, take note of what you already do to assess your leadership impact, and notice what new actions might be available to you.

Gathering Feedback

There are three ways you can gather feedback from others:

1. Solicit feedback from a trusted mentor, confidant, or coach
2. Participate in an anonymous 360-degree feedback assessment
3. Solicit face-to-face feedback on a regular basis from your colleagues and employees

Having a trusted mentor or coach can be an invaluable source of feedback, as it was for our client Jim. If you don't have a mentor or coach inside or outside of your organization—someone to whom you can turn for feedback, confidential counsel, and encouragement—we recommend that you find one. Leadership can be a difficult and lonely endeavor; the best leaders realize this and get the support they need to excel.

In addition to an ongoing relationship with a mentor or coach, you can gather feedback from others through the use of anonymous feedback surveys. Many leaders have participated in 360-degree feedback processes that are offered through their organizations, and there are many good instruments out there now for this purpose. In addition to using an online instrument, we've found it useful to sit down with leaders and generate a list of feedback questions that are customized to them, along with a list of people whose opinions and assessments they value. We then interview those people and share the salient feedback themes with our clients.

We believe strongly that any 360-degree feedback process should help you better see your strengths and the positive impact you have on others, in addition to shedding light on where you can do better. On page 209 in the appendix, we've included a list of the most impactful questions we've uncovered over the years when gathering 360-degree feedback for our clients. You'll see that the first two questions are geared toward strengths and ask for examples of the positive difference you've made for others when you've been at your best.

These 360-degree assessments can be helpful at many junctures in your development as a leader, but we especially recommend them when you have taken on a new role or you are leading your team or organization in a new direction. The feedback can be instrumental in helping you see where you are making progress and where you may need to step it up to succeed.

Finally, soliciting feedback face-to-face from colleagues and employees is perhaps the most valuable method of the three we listed earlier. Why? You can employ this strategy as frequently as needed, and it sets a powerful example for others to follow. We recommend that you consider building this kind of upward feedback into your performance appraisals process and into your status meetings and check-ins. One client we know ends every evaluation and quarterly check-in with his employees by asking them two questions:

1. Where can *I* do better?

2. How can I better support *you*?

This same client asks one or two trusted colleagues to give him feedback after key internal meetings on how well he is embodying his Impact Statement. Because he has a track record of listening openly to their feedback, they actually give it to him.

Making it safe for people to give you feedback is key. Most people tread very lightly when it comes to giving their bosses feedback. Here are a few tips that we've found to be helpful in creating a safe environment for people to tell you the truth:

1. Don't wait for people to give you feedback. Seek it out yourself using one of the ideas suggested earlier. Only then will you demonstrate that you are genuinely interested and open to hearing it.

2. Whenever you do receive feedback, even if you disagree with it, thank people for their willingness to share it with you and resist getting defensive. It doesn't matter if you are right and they are wrong; what you're trying to do is signal your willingness to hear tough messages, even those with which you disagree.

3. Don't shy away from giving feedback to those who report to you, both positive and negative, and model how to do it well. If you aren't giving direct reports regular feedback, it will be even less likely that they'll take the risk of giving it to you.

4. Find some way to take action on the feedback you receive. People will always believe your actions more than your words.

Developing Your "Observer Muscle"

In addition to gathering feedback from others, you can also assess your impact by stepping into what we call the *observer mode.* Think of the observer mode as a built-in tool for giving yourself feedback when the game is on and you need to be at your best.

In their book *Leadership on the Line,* authors Heifetz and Linsky call this act of reflecting in the midst of action "getting off the dance floor and going to the balcony."[2] Getting on the balcony can be a useful metaphor for envisioning how you step back from what you're doing, while you're doing it, to see yourself from a new perspective and adjust your actions accordingly.

For many people, the observer muscle is underdeveloped, and strengthening it requires conscious intention, effort, and practice. While many leaders understand the importance of observing or noticing the impact of their *actions,* what is less understood is the value of observing three other elements that impact our leadership presence and affect how others see us:

- Our moods and emotions
- Our language (both our spoken words as well as our thoughts and internal dialogue)
- Our physical comportment (our posture and the way we "carry" ourselves)

Observing all three of these elements and, of course, correcting them when needed can pay big dividends, as it did for our client Erica. As you read her story, consider how becoming a more astute observer of your mood, language, and posture might also benefit you.

Giving Resignation the Boot: Erica's Story

Erica was the director of business development for a growing division of a large food services company. She was selected for this newly created role because of her extensive résumé and was expected to use her expertise to make significant changes in her new company's marketing strategy.

However, six months into her new role, Erica was struggling. At key meetings where she was supposed to be enrolling people in her new initiatives, Erica found that she was routinely ignored or dismissed by her more assertive and aggressive colleagues. Erica didn't feel like her peers treated her as an equal partner at the table, and she was growing increasingly discouraged as a result. As is often the case, the more discouraged she became, the harder it was for her to show up confidently and powerfully with her peers.

Erica's boss decided she could use the support of a coach and hired us to help change the downward spiral in which she found herself. But every time we suggested an idea about how she might alter her situation for the better, Erica would respond with some version of "I've tried that already and it doesn't work" or "There's really nothing I can do to change the way these people are here. They never listen to anyone." This is the language of resignation. When we're in this mood, the story we tell ourselves is, "Why bother?" We believe that nothing we do or say will make any difference.

Erica's resignation even showed up in her body and overall comportment. Erica sat slightly slumped, with a rounded spine and shoulders. She also held her head tilted to one side, which gave her the appearance of being unsure of herself. In addition to these postural tendencies, Erica wore a large fleece jacket in the office when she was cold. It covered her up and concealed the fact that under that jacket, she was a very well-dressed woman. All of this added up to a less than credible presence. Erica wasn't taken seriously, and neither was her team. The situation was so bad that she was considering resigning.

With her permission, we shared our observations and assessments. We focused particularly on the way she tended to slump in her chair. As she straightened her spine, opened up across her shoulders, and sat up taller, she immediately noticed a difference. "I already feel like I have more authority," she told us.

We invited Erica to confront her mood of resignation head-on and to decide for herself whether she wanted to continue in her current role. After some reflection, Erica decided to stay and to commit to making a bigger difference where she was. Realizing that she had a choice and exercising it helped her to move out of resignation and into a mood of ambition and possibility.

Erica agreed to observe both her tendency to slump at meetings and her inner dialogue of "why bother" for the next several weeks. Whenever she caught herself in a posture or thought pattern that wasn't consistent with the impact she wanted to have, she would adjust it accordingly. She also agreed to only wear her fleece jacket if she was in her office by herself.

When we saw Erica again, we were immediately struck by the change in her demeanor. She appeared more confident and energized. She shared with us how she had caught herself slumping several times in key meetings with stakeholders and staff, and how sitting up had helped her to reengage in the conversations from a place of greater strength. She also caught herself when she started to complain to her staff about her colleagues and instead redirected the conversation to a more fruitful place. She hadn't once worn her fleece jacket around the office and was getting compliments again on her style and dress.

While these changes may seem like small adjustments, to Erica, they added up to a big difference in how she felt, and that translated into a big difference in how she came across to her team and her colleagues. Not only was she showing up more confidently and credibly at work, but the shifts in her posture and mood were having a positive impact on the home front, where her husband and son noticed the change as well.

Your Turn, Part 1: The Power of Posture

Erica's story reveals how mood is reflected in language and how it shapes the way you carry yourself. And the reverse is also true: the way you carry yourself shapes your mood. To experience this firsthand, try this exercise:

- Slump over in your chair, allowing your shoulders to round in and your spine to collapse. Exaggerate this motion by leaning over your knees and allowing your hands to fall forward toward the ground and your chin to touch your chest. From this slumped position, imagine selling an important idea or advocating for yourself. What do you notice?

- Now shake that position off and lengthen your spine. Sit up tall, open up across your chest, and tilt your chin slightly up. Allow a subtle smile to form. Again, imagine selling an important idea or advocating for something you're passionate about. What do you notice about your ability to speak confidently from this posture?

Your Turn, Part 2: Mood Matters

Moods form the emotional backdrop to your life and your leadership. Like Erica, you can fall into a particular mood and not even be aware of it. Use the following questions to think about your mood(s) as a leader and their impact on those around you:

1. In which mood (or combination of moods) do you find yourself these days? Is this mood helping you to have the impact you desire, or is it hindering you? (For more information on moods, see "Common Moods and Their Impact" on page 211 in the appendix.)

2. Some moods, like optimism and curiosity, tend to be more resourceful. Others, like resignation, anxiety, or resentment, tend to interfere with a team's productivity and performance. What mood or combination of moods do you see in your team right now? How might your mood be impacting theirs?

Next time you find yourself or your team in a mood that is interfering with your productivity or performance, consider using one of the following strategies to shift it.

Change your posture and the way you carry yourself. Sometimes the quickest way to shift your mood is to make a change in the way you are sitting, standing, walking, or breathing.

Tell a different story. Your mood is held in place or supported by an internal narrative, or story, which often lies just beneath your conscious awareness. Listen for the story you are telling yourself or others about your present situation. Is it a story that empowers you? If not, change it to one that does.

Inject humor and playfulness. You can't do your best thinking when you're tense, taking yourself too seriously, or anxious. Find ways to be playful, to introduce humor, and to laugh with your team. Doing so can immediately change the tone of a meeting and help to create an environment that supports creative problem solving.

Exercise. Most of the executives we have worked with have found a way to fit exercise into their daily routine. Exercise releases endorphins and is known to improve not only physical health but also mental and emotional well-being. When you find yourself in a mood that doesn't support what you want to accomplish, consider taking a brisk walk or engaging in some other form of exercise. Physical activity is a potent mood shifter. See chapter 5 for additional information on the benefits of exercise.

Speak with grounded optimism. Grounded optimism is the unwavering belief that you can and will prevail, balanced by a clear sense of the obstacles ahead and a game plan for dealing with them. Identify the reasons for being hopeful about the future and back them up with realistic goals and a concrete plan. For more information about this, see chapter 7.

Express appreciation or gratitude. Next time you find yourself in a mood that is limiting your energy or impact, take a minute to think about the people around you who have contributed to your success or have made your life easier or more fulfilling. Take a few minutes to send a personalized note to thank them for their contribution or tell them in person. Expressing appreciation lifts the mood of both the sender and the receiver.

Phase 3: Close the Gap

If you've arrived at this point in the chapter—and have undertaken the reflections and suggestions we've offered so far—you now have a clear Impact Statement describing the leader you aspire to be. Chances are you've also begun to see more clearly the gaps between how you want to impact others and how you actually do. Now we turn our attention to how you can close these gaps and, in doing so, have greater influence and credibility in your organization.

Jim and Erica's stories in the previous section reveal how powerful it can be to become a better observer of your pace, your posture, and your mood. For this reason, developing your observer muscle, *and course correcting on the spot as needed,* is not only a way to uncover gaps; it is also an invaluable tool for closing them.

In this section, we offer you two additional strategies for managing your impact and closing your leadership gaps:

1. Develop a "Stop, Start, and Keep Doing" Action Plan: Identify one thing you will *stop* doing, one thing you will *start* doing, and one thing you will *keep* doing to more fully embody your Impact Statement and to respond to any feedback you receive. Decide on the routines and supporting practices that will enable you to take these actions and develop them into habits.

2. Manage the shadow side of your strengths: Uncover whether some of your greatest strengths are actually working against you and limiting your impact—either because you are applying them without discernment or because others are misinterpreting them. Adjust how you deploy your strengths accordingly.

We'll elaborate in just a bit on what we mean by the "shadow side" of your strengths. For now, let's take a closer look at the first strategy by returning to Sam's story.

From Insight to Action: Sam's Story

Sam's Impact Statement reflected a growing realization that he needed to inspire more and intimidate less. As soon as he was reconnected with this vision of how he wanted to be as a leader, Sam made some immediate course corrections.

First, he made a commitment to stop raising his voice and berating people. When he could feel himself getting frustrated or disappointed by those he led, he took a deep breath, paused, and remembered his Impact Statement. He also shared his Impact Statement with his closest ally and confidant. If he slipped and fell back into his old habits, he gave this person permission to call him on it. When this happened, Sam acknowledged it and, in some cases, apologized.

A few months after making these initial course corrections, Sam agreed to have us collect 360-degree feedback for him. We sat down to debrief the feedback with him, which contained both positive encouragement and constructive criticism.

His employees' examples of him at his best were positive and profound. Many of his direct reports commented that they owed much of who they were as professionals and as people to Sam and the mentoring they had received from him over the years. Others spoke of his visionary strengths and the bold leadership he had exhibited at key times in the life of the company. These positive messages about Sam's impact inspired him to rise up and fulfill his own potential as a leader.

His colleagues also mentioned that they had noticed Sam's efforts to practice greater emotional restraint. They appreciated that he was making a concerted effort to refrain from raising his voice and knew how difficult this was for him. Hearing this encouraged Sam, and he committed to keep doing this, even though it required a great deal of effort and attention on his part.

Sam's colleagues also shared a few things he was doing that eroded his effectiveness and impact. For example, he learned that his subordinates were uncomfortable when he shared information about other employees with them. Sam also learned that he wasn't providing enough clarity around the future direction of the company. Finally, he discovered that his mentoring abilities and visionary boldness were not being utilized fully. On the basis of the feedback and the changes he had already begun to make, we suggested Sam create a "Stop, Start, and Keep Doing" Action Plan, in which he identified specific commitments to improve his leadership. This simple process helped Sam to continue on his journey of becoming the leader he envisioned himself to be and provided a concrete plan to which he could refer on a daily or weekly basis.

Your Turn

1. Sam was able to course correct in part because he gave permission to one of his colleagues to give him feedback on a recurring basis. Is there a trusted colleague with whom you could share your Impact Statement—someone you could ask to give you targeted feedback on how well you are embodying it on a daily basis? If so, resolve to share your Impact Statement with that person today.

2. In light of your self-observations thus far (and any feedback you may have gathered from colleagues), what is one thing you could *stop doing,* one thing you could *keep doing,* and one thing you could *start doing* to be more impactful in your leadership? Capture your answers in writing and review your action plan weekly.

Managing the Shadow Side of Your Strengths

Before we conclude this chapter, let's return again to this key strategy for closing the gap between the leader you want to be and the leader that others see. Some of your greatest strengths can work against you, eroding your impact and credibility. This happens when people experience the shadow side of your strengths—either because you are overusing them or because you are deploying them without awareness or finesse. To have the kind of positive impact you desire, it's important to know which of your strengths might be getting in your way and how to better manage them if they are.

As you consider your top two or three strengths, is there a shadow side to them that could be limiting your impact in some way? If you have a commanding presence, for example, do you sometimes come across as bossy or arrogant? Is empathy one of your gifts? If so, does your talent for understanding how others feel prevent you from making tough people decisions? What about a keen analytical mind? If you possess one, do you sometimes get lost in the minutiae of problems, delving so deeply into them that you lose sight of the broader vision?

Ask colleagues, family members, or friends who know you best to help you identify the shadow side of your strengths and the impact they have on others. Then be sure to observe your strengths in action and notice if, or when, the shadow side is coming through. Your strengths should be working for you, not against you.

The Impact Conversation: Key Takeaways

The further you move up in an organization, the more insulated you become. By engaging in the Impact Conversation, you entered into a conversation about how you impact others and explored ways to escape the isolation of this perilous bubble. You declared your intended impact when you developed a clear and compelling Impact Statement that will serve as a touchstone for your leadership in the days ahead. You faced your blind spots with courage and resolve and persisted in gathering feedback from those who see you in action. You've exercised your "observer muscle" so you can better read and gauge your impact in the moment and course correct as necessary. And you've considered how those strengths you count on, when overused, can undermine your desired impact. When you said yes to this conversation, you became a powerful model in your organization for transparency, openness, and trust.

The Impact Conversation: What's Next?

Coaching Assignments for Leveraging Your Learning

Is the Impact Conversation particularly critical for you? The following list of Actions, Practices, and Resources is a tool kit for engaging more deeply in this important Missing Conversation.

Action Steps

- Ensure that your leadership Impact Statement comes alive in your leadership practice by completing the Impact Statement and Actions Worksheet on page 213 in the appendix. Check in with your progress each day.
- If you haven't done so recently, participate in a 360-degree feedback process. Consider having someone in HR or an outside coach

collect feedback for you using some or all of the questions we've listed on page 209 in the appendix.

- Ask a trusted colleague to tell you the unvarnished truth about how you are coming across to others. Receive this response as a gift.

Ongoing Practices

- Start your day by reviewing your leadership Impact Statement, and read it aloud to yourself. Notice your energy level as you do.
- Twice a day, hit the pause button and ask yourself, "What's my mood right now?" Notice how it is impacting your performance and reflect on how it might be impacting your team. Do what you need to shift it, if necessary.
- At least once every quarter, ask those who work for you two simple questions: (1) How am I doing? and (2) What can I do to better support you? Act on what you hear.

Suggested Resources

Leadership on the Line: Staying Alive through the Dangers of Leading by Ronald A. Heifetz and Marty Linsky: Harvard Business School Press, 2002.

"Stop Overdoing Your Strengths" by Robert E. Kaplan and Robert B. Kaiser: *Harvard Business Review*, February 2009.

What Got You Here, Won't Get You There by Marshall Goldsmith: Hyperion Books, 2007.

CHAPTER 3

What Provokes Me and How Do I React? The Triggers Conversation

Every moment in which we are caught—by desire, by an emotion, by an unexamined impulse, idea or opinion—in a very real way, we are instantly imprisoned by the habitual ways in which we react.

—Jon Kabat-Zinn, *Arriving at Your Own Front Door: 108 Lessons in Mindfulness*

When the stakes are high, how do you maintain your equilibrium and recover from the unexpected? Is it possible for you to respond thoughtfully rather than react mindlessly when you're provoked? Can you lead with less reactivity and greater equanimity? These are the questions that consume many of the leaders with whom we work. Like you, they crave the capacity to remain calm and balanced in their reactions to challenging people and circumstances. They want to be able to manage themselves well and inspire calm and clear thinking in others.

Because human beings are biologically hardwired to react, this goal can feel unreachable at times. Certain situations or people invite your reactivity and override your aspiration for skillful self-control—even when those situations demand highly professional behavior. A client of ours, a nurse manager, recently shared an example of reactivity that seemed too outrageous to believe. A new operating room tech had accidentally handed the wrong surgical instrument to a surgeon—who then threw the instrument at her in a rage. Whereas we were astonished, our client shrugged in resignation. This kind of reaction among some of her surgeons, though not routine, was not atypical.

You've likely witnessed examples of people who, when provoked, become unhinged—literally disconnected from their calm center. They react forcefully and in a way that seems out of proportion given the triggering person or circumstances. In the grip of their strong emotions, they find themselves overreacting in the moment, often with disastrous consequences.

Like most people, you can probably point to situations in your own past where you've responded emotionally to triggers in ways that separated you from your calm and centered self. Your emotional reactions hijacked you—possibly with damaging results. As social scientist Paul Ekman notes in his book *Emotions Revealed,* these experiences of emotional reactivity are troubling and leave an unpleasant residue. You may realize in retrospect that the intensity of your reaction didn't match with what was called for in the situation; or you might have felt the right emotion but expressed it in the wrong way. Afterward, you might find yourself attempting to explain away your behavior, ignoring it altogether, or apologizing profusely for it later.[1]

Some leaders with whom we work insist that they're able to stifle their reactivity and hide it successfully from others. When triggered, they explain, their reactivity turns inward. Like many people, they believe that if they don't explode outwardly and are somehow able to mask their reactions, they'll magically make those reactions disappear. Still other leaders with whom we work aren't even aware of their reactivity. One leader we coached showed few visible signs of reactivity, but her direct reports and peers all knew when she was triggered. When people or situations knocked her off balance, her default response was to shut down and pull away from others. Although she didn't have outbursts, her reactive cutoffs were equally as damaging to her public image.

Your nervous system doesn't give you much latitude for ignoring your triggers. Though you may not react explosively to something that triggers you, your body can't help but respond. You may clench your jaw, unconsciously ball your fists, or contract your shoulders—physical reactions that are apparent to others, even if you're unaware of them. You can slip unconsciously into a response pattern that harms your relationships and undermines your influence.

Although most people can point to trigger scenarios in their own lives, fewer understand why they get triggered in the first place. You might easily recall the physical and emotional experience of being knocked off center but struggle to articulate why you responded in the way that you did. In hindsight, you might describe the scenario as a moment in time when you simply weren't "yourself."

After the fact, you can find yourself steeped in regret or embarrassment about your reaction and concerned that your response has provoked unnecessary negative fallout. But you're unable to make sense of your reactions. Why did you lose your ability to reason in the moment and to respond in a thoughtful way? Can you learn how to manage your reactivity differently?

Our coaching clients engage in the Triggers Conversation because they've noticed a pattern of reactivity that's eroding their working relationships, their well-being, and their effectiveness. They may also launch into the conversation because a badly handled scenario continues to haunt them. Understanding what happened and why becomes essential if they are to shake off the toxic residue of self-recrimination and remorse the situation has left behind. As they step back and honestly assess their leadership, they recognize that learning how to respond differently when triggered and how to recover more nimbly requires a new level of self-exploration and self-management.

What's the cost to you when you're frequently triggered and aren't able to easily recover your calm? Reactivity inevitably produces breakdowns and escalates conflict. Getting caught in your triggers' grip can damage your relationships, both at work and at home, and compromise your impact as a leader. As we discuss in both our Impact Conversation and Well-Being Conversation chapters, your mood as a leader is infectious. The quality of your presence either calms others or invites their reactivity. A pattern of reactivity, or being frequently triggered, affects the quality of your presence and sabotages your success as a leader.

But you don't have to reexperience the same pattern of reactivity when your triggers show up. In this chapter, we'll guide you through three phases of self-discovery that will lead you to a deepened awareness of your triggers and an improved capacity to recover more skillfully when you're provoked.

PHASE 1: NAME YOUR TRIGGERS

Demonizing your triggers will only bring you heartache and tighten their grip. If you treat them with curiosity, you can examine them with more distance and perspective. When you explore the mysterious territory of what provokes you and how, you open yourself up to transformational learning and sustainable change. Once you step into this process of naming your triggers and holding them up to the light of day without judgment, you unlock new possibilities for responding to situations or people. Your capacity to lead and influence others will grow as you develop insight into your reactive tendencies and explore strategies for working with them.

Confronting your triggers requires courage and faith: courage to explore a territory that's often confusing and scary and faith that shifts in your behavior are possible when you face what's present and true for you. Our clients' journeys remind us that great leadership requires looking inward and accepting the unvarnished version of ourselves with compassion and understanding.

The clients we profile in this chapter are conscientious leaders. They genuinely care about the people they manage and are deeply committed to leading effectively. In our coaching conversations, they recognized that their habit of reactivity was undermining the quality of their relationships at work and compromising their success. As you read their stories, ask yourself how you might benefit from identifying your triggers, recognizing your reactions, and managing them more skillfully.

Taking Ownership: Suzanne's Story

An experienced senior leader and clinician, Suzanne had worked successfully in the health care field for her entire career. She was comfortable voicing her opinions and held firm to her positions when clinical issues were on the table for discussion. As she joined her boss and colleagues for their weekly executive team meeting, she readied herself to take a strong stand on a decision that would directly impact her clinical staff. As she voiced her point of view in the meeting, Rick, the CFO, interrupted her and asked her questions that seemed designed to undermine her credibility. She felt her blood begin to boil as soon as he spoke. This was not the first time that Rick had challenged her in front of her boss and colleagues. She lashed out at Rick, accusing him of intentionally questioning her leadership. An awkward silence swallowed the team. She felt embarrassed by her behavior and victimized by Rick. "How in the world," she wondered, "do I recover from this one?"

Suzanne reached out to us for leadership coaching with a deep desire to make a shift in her relationship with Rick. The public outburst she'd had in her executive team meeting had left her feeling bruised and confused, but she recognized that she couldn't expect Rick to change. If she wanted their conversations to be different, she needed to understand her reactions and learn how to manage them in the moment more successfully.

In our coaching conversations, Suzanne stepped back from the triggering incident and acknowledged that she and Rick shared a history of misunderstanding and tense interactions. She perceived him as closed and distant, unwilling to respect her point of view and dismissive of her team. As we processed her experiences with Rick, she realized that when he challenged her ideas, either privately or publicly, she felt he was challenging her expertise.

The more he pushed back on her positions or recommendations, the more certain she became that he discounted her skills and contributions. Once this interpretation took hold, she felt hurt and devalued. Wounded, she would lash back out at him, and their communication would spiral downward.

Once she had clarified for herself that it was her story, or interpretation, of Rick's behavior that provoked her anger, she could let go of some of her resentment and begin to see his style for what it was: a preference for challenging any positions to arrive at the most financially sound decision possible. His behavior toward her wasn't personal, but she had responded to it as if it were.

With this newly discovered insight, Suzanne could better recognize when she was jumping to this interpretation and catch herself consciously before it overtook her and provoked a negative response. She learned to be on alert for a tightening in her chest as a physical warning sign that she was triggered and then would intentionally deepen her breath to calm her reactivity. She adopted a new practice for her conversations with Rick. She would ask herself what assumptions she was making about Rick's intentions and noticed that when she paused in this way, she could remain in conversation with him without seething inside. She was able to hear his point of view without getting defensive. Suzanne realized that her story about Rick had invited her to build a wall of defensiveness and shut down to his views and positions. She recognized that the most useful strategy she could deploy to improve her interactions with Rick or anyone else was to acknowledge and manage her triggers consciously.

Your Turn

Find a space where you can reflect undisturbed on the following questions.

1. Recall the last time you were significantly triggered. Immerse yourself in the details of the experience.
    - Who or what triggered you?
    - What emotions did you experience?
    - How did you react?
    - What was the impact of your response?

- How long did it take you to regain your balance?

2. Do you wish you had responded differently? How would you like to have responded?
3. Take a look at the Common Triggers Checklist. Which ones are true for you? Identify your top three.

Common Triggers Checklist

Here's a list of situations that often provoke an immediate physiological response and emotional reaction in the leaders we coach. Notice which of these are triggers for you, too.

- ☐ Requests or demands that are issued without an appreciation of what's already on your plate
- ☐ Being left out of the loop on important e-mails or meetings
- ☐ People not showing up to meetings on time
- ☐ Being disrespected by your peers or boss in front of others
- ☐ Having your credibility or expertise questioned
- ☐ Being interrupted repeatedly
- ☐ E-mail communication that discusses sensitive matters that would be better handled in person
- ☐ Someone taking credit for others' work or failing to acknowledge the work of others
- ☐ When someone misses a deadline to which he or she had agreed without notifying you in advance
- ☐ Not being acknowledged for a job well done
- ☐ When people bring you their problems without a proposed solution
- ☐ Meetings that go on and on with no clear agenda or agreements made

When revisiting past experiences of being provoked, you may find yourself wondering why certain circumstances or people knock you off balance but don't seem to affect others around you in the same way. As a leader, you may have found yourself provoked by a particular person or event when others on your team seemed unfazed. How do you explain these different responses?

Understanding your own unique triggers and distinguishing them from triggers that are shared more universally will help you anticipate situations that are likely to provoke you and enable you to respond to them more thoughtfully.

In his book *Emotions Revealed,* Ekman distinguishes between two types of emotional triggers. *Autoappraisers* are those types of circumstances that trigger reactivity in most, if not all, of us. When a person cuts us off in traffic, for instance, we feel thwarted in our attempt to move forward. When we feel thwarted, most of us will experience anger and frustration or even a desire for retribution.

Ekman describes another type of emotional trigger, the *individual trigger*. These are situations or types of people that are unique triggers for you. They are the triggers that result from your personal experiences, often from childhood, and provoke strong emotions in you without a clear understanding as to why. We're all vulnerable to triggers that remind us of painful or confusing experiences. Becoming more conscious of your individualized triggers will be particularly helpful for you as a leader as you seek to be a calm presence in your organization. Understanding the triggers that are uniquely yours will enable you to anticipate and minimize their negative influence. Equipped with greater self-awareness, you'll be able to self-regulate more skillfully when these triggers show up in your life and leadership.

Whether the trigger you explored in the "*Your Turn*" section of this chapter was individual or autoappraisal, the experience of being provoked is typically the same. It's helpful to understand and distinguish between the various stages of being triggered. Though these stages essentially happen simultaneously, naming and distinguishing them can be a useful tool for finding new ways to disrupt their negative impact. When sharing these stages of reactivity with our clients, we refer to it as the Sequence of Reactivity.

SEQUENCE OF REACTIVITY

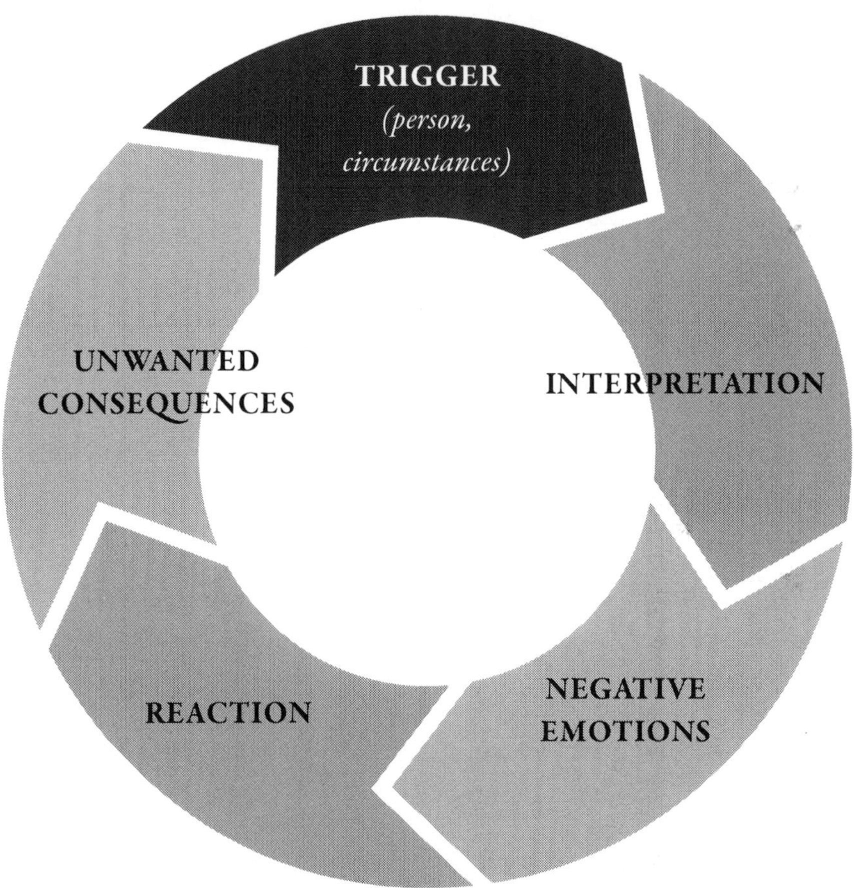

Recall the last time you were reactive. If you step far enough back from your experience, as if you were a witness to yourself being triggered, you're likely to notice that you experienced the triggering circumstances or person who provoked you first as unpleasant. You then attached a particular meaning to what provoked you, likely based on past experiences or associations, and this interpretation evoked strong negative emotions. Your emotions influenced how you responded, and your responses may have unleashed consequences that you later regretted.

When you recognize the Sequence of Reactivity for what it is—a predictable pattern of trigger responses—you'll learn that through intentional self-observation and practice, you can intervene early on in the Sequence and interrupt it. You don't have to be held hostage by your reactions. You can ask yourself simple questions that transport you from the part of your brain responsible for reactivity to your prefrontal cortex, or executive functioning brain. Once this shift has happened, you are no longer in the grip of reactivity and are able to think more clearly and respond more thoughtfully to what or who is provoking you.

Imagine that a direct report of yours hasn't delivered on a commitment. Your first reaction is to feel enraged. How could he have failed to deliver on time for such an important client? You storm toward his office ready to lay into him, muttering expletives as you march down the hallway. If you burst into his office in the grip of your reactivity, what results are you likely to get? Defensiveness? Stonewalling? Reciprocal outrage?

What if you took a few seconds to pause and ask yourself the following questions:

- What am I assuming right now about this situation? About this person?
- What emotion am I feeling right now? How will this emotion impact my actions?
- What's the result I want from this confrontation?

Questions like these are a remarkable antidote to reactivity. Once you interrupt your Sequence of Reactivity, you have more choice about your responses. You can better recognize in the moment that what feels real to you is not necessarily true. When you build the muscle of self-control, you build the capacity to regain your calm, even in the face of triggers that have provoked you in the past.

Phase 2: Observe Your Reactions

The simple act of naming what hijacks you can loosen your triggers' hold and facilitate a shift in how you respond when you're provoked. Building a different kind of relationship with your triggers, whether they are a specific set of circumstances or particular types of people, becomes possible when you've done the work to identify them and trained yourself to observe them in action. Like letting go of an old friend who you realize is no longer good for you, recognizing and relating to your triggers in a new way can invite both relief and renewal.

But old habits of reactivity die hard. Your brain and body are locked into certain patterns of interpreting and responding to triggers, and these patterns can be challenging to change. If you've ever tried giving up coffee, smoking cigarettes, or any habit that's not serving you, you know firsthand how difficult it can be to let go of a behavior that's become habitual. You have to become hypervigilant. Without rigorous self-awareness and self-management, a pattern of reactivity, just like any other ingrained habit, can seem impossible to overcome.

Physical reactions are the first sign that you are triggered. When you make sense of a situation or someone else's behavior in a way that provokes a particular story, that story lives in your nervous system and invites a physical response. Like an early warning weather system, your physical sensations give you notice that you're about to slip into reactivity.

Paying attention to these signals produced invaluable insights that enabled our client, Bob, to respond thoughtfully versus reacting negatively to his new team member, Jennifer. As you read his story, consider how becoming more observant of your bodily sensations could equip you to work with your reactivity more skillfully.

Listening to the Body: Bob's Story

Bob was an executive in a consulting firm with an extraordinary level of dedication to his team's mission and his staff's success. His department was renowned for its expertise, its customer service, and the talent of its team members. He was passionate about cultivating excellence in his team and hired carefully when opportunities emerged to grow his staff. He prided himself on selecting new team members who would complement the staff's set of strengths and was not afraid to hire someone who brought a different viewpoint or approach.

Recently, Bob contacted us for coaching support when he began to run into conflict with his newest hire, Jennifer. He admitted that the conflict, though low level, was eating away at him and provoking some anxiety that he couldn't quite understand. As we discussed his challenge, we launched into the Triggers Conversation and began to examine the nature of his conflict with Jennifer and what it revealed about his triggers.

Bob acknowledged that he felt tense and on alert in both one-on-one and group meetings with Jennifer. He left his conversations with her feeling ill at ease and anxious, but he wasn't clear why. The more discomfort he felt in her presence, the more frustrated he became with himself and the situation. His emotional response to Jennifer was shaping the quality of their interactions, and he feared it would begin to negatively influence his team. With openness and courage, he began to unbundle his reactions and arrive at some clarity about what triggered him about their relationship and communication.

Arriving at this clarity meant that Bob needed to understand his emotions and their connection to his responses. It wouldn't be enough for him to commit to new ways of interacting with Jennifer. He would need to shine a light on the emotional triggers that were driving his current reactions before he could expect himself to behave differently. We invited him to explore the physical experience of his reactivity first.

We asked Bob to remember the circumstances surrounding his latest interaction with Jennifer. He recalled that she had challenged him once again on an important decision that he had already revisited with her numerous times. We asked him to remember the physical sensations that accompanied his conversation with her. He recalled that he had felt queasy and his fists had clenched when they launched back into an argument over a decision he wasn't willing to reverse.

We encouraged him to slip back into his physical experience and revisit the queasiness he'd felt. He recognized that his physical responses were indicators of panic. Acknowledging the panic enabled him to recognize a story that he'd been afraid to face: the thought that Jennifer might be a poor fit for his team's culture. He prided himself on the respectful and supportive climate they'd created and noted that Jennifer's abrasive and argumentative approach conflicted with his team's norms for managing disagreements. He realized that the notion that he may have made a mistake in hiring Jennifer was driving him to do everything possible to accommodate her and tolerate behaviors he would never tolerate in another team member.

Bob prided himself on his hiring acumen and acknowledged that admitting a hiring mistake was difficult. He believed his team depended on him to make flawless hiring decisions. When he allowed himself to focus on the physical sensations associated with his interactions with Jennifer, he connected with his panic and the thinking or story beneath his panic. Touching that experience of panic unlocked a revelation about his reactivity and enabled him to admit that he needed to address his concerns with Jennifer and her approach openly and directly.

Bob sat down with Jennifer and raised his specific concerns about her behavior in meetings and her interactions with their team. He shared his perspective on the impact of her communication style and outlined the shifts he needed her to make to blend successfully with the team. Once he had connected with his body's wisdom, he was able to see clearly that he'd been accommodating Jennifer in a way that compromised his expectations and vision for his team.

Your Turn

You'll need a tranquil space to reflect on the following questions. Give yourself enough uninterrupted time to quiet your mind and your body before responding to these inquiries.

1. Recall a recent experience when you were triggered, either at work or at home. Acclimate yourself to that experience: close your eyes; picture the person or people involved; revisit the circumstances as

if you were watching a video feed of the incident. Immerse yourself in your memory of the event. Once you've revisited this experience, ask yourself the following:

- What sensations did you notice in your body?
- What part of your body, if any, contracted or tightened as you recalled this experience?
- Focus your attention on that area of your body.
- What sensations are you aware of now?
- What emotions are you feeling now as you focus your attention on those areas of your body?
- What wisdom or message do your physical sensations offer you about what provokes you, and why?

2. Take a look at the following list of possible responses from the book *Resilient Leadership* that you may see in yourself when you're provoked. Which pattern of reactivity tends to show up most often for you?[2]

   ☐ I tend to get frustrated and combative with others.
   ☐ I tend to withdraw and avoid contact with others.
   ☐ I tend to mask my reaction and shut down to the situation.
   ☐ I tend to seek peace at any cost.

While many of us tend to live in our heads and value our intellect above all else, our self includes a physical body as well as a brain, and the two are inextricably connected through our nervous system. Our conditioned tendency when triggered is hardwired into our nervous system and informs our reactive behavior. Although we experience all four types of reactivity (fight, flight, freeze, or appease) depending on the circumstances, one tendency is more pronounced in our repertoire and tends to show up more often.

With increased self-awareness of your own conditioned response to triggers, you can exercise more choice and control over your pattern of reacting. Your body can become your ally when you're in the throes of reactivity. When you name where and how reactivity is showing up in your body, you can contain it more successfully.

Bringing your focused attention more routinely to your body can help you build a closer relationship to your nervous system and train you to be on the lookout for early signals of reactivity. Take a moment now to shift your attention to your physical body. Notice the sensations associated with being seated. Feel the connection between your feet and the floor. Experience the texture of your socks or shoes or the sensation of the soles of your feet touching the ground. Now let your attention sweep upward from your feet to the crown of your head. What sensations are you aware of in your body? Where are your muscles contracted or holding tension?

Understanding your brain's biology as well, even in the most basic way, provides insight into your behavior when you're triggered and suggests a road map for managing your tendencies when you're provoked. When faced with a threat, the most primitive part of your brain, your limbic system, shifts into overdrive. This part of your brain, which some researchers refer to as the "reptilian" brain, gave prehistoric humans the ability to be on the alert for constant threats to their survival. This part of your brain is constantly scanning for external threats and messaging to your nervous system when one appears. Unfortunately, your limbic system doesn't know how to distinguish between a panther lying in wait to devour you for lunch and any other circumstances or people you might experience as harmful.

Once in the grip of your limbic system, you lose touch with your higher reasoning self, your prefrontal cortex, and fall victim to a triggered reactive response that you'll probably recognize as fight, flight, freeze, or appease. Your body wants to fight the situation or person who's provoked you; run away to avoid the trigger at all costs; collapse in helplessness; or make nice in the situation in an effort to unload the anxiety that the triggering situation or person has provoked.

Although you likely face triggers that are far less severe than those faced by early humans, your primal brain still influences your nervous system, and your body reads the signals it sends with instantaneous precision.

Your heart beats more quickly to pump blood toward your major muscle groups so you can fight or run, and hormones like adrenaline and cortisol are released to sharpen your reflexes. None of these physical responses to triggers is designed to help you reason in the moment; rather, they prepare you to respond to a threat in a way that will ensure your survival.

When you're in the Sequence of Reactivity, your body is trained to follow the lead of your nervous system. If you don't want your triggers to drive your responses, you need to develop a more intimate connection to the signals your body is sending you and increase your awareness of your fight, flight, freeze, or appease tendencies. As a leader, your ability to attune yourself to your tendencies through your awareness of your body's signals will enable you to consciously choose your responses to your triggers with greater ease and skill. Though not an easy task, reading your body's messages can be the first and most essential step in rewiring your habitual responses to your triggers.[3]

PHASE 3: REGAIN YOUR CENTER

The latest neuroscience research holds encouraging news for all of us. Recent experiments point to the malleable nature of our brains and the capacity we have to develop new neural pathways through intentional focus and practice. Through repeated experiments using brain imaging, researchers like Dr. Jeffrey Schwartz, a psychiatrist at UCLA School of Medicine, are demonstrating and documenting the brain's plasticity and its ability to establish new neural pathways that result in changed behaviors over time.[4] Recent data suggest that we are more capable of making sustainable behavioral changes than researchers previously thought.

What might this mean for you in relationship to your own reactivity? How might you intentionally rewire your neural pathways to recover more easily when you're triggered?

Our client Janet's experience illustrates the powerful impact of practice on our ability to manage ourselves more effectively and recover more easily when we're caught in the grip of reactivity.

Recovering Equilibrium: Janet's Story

Janet, a federal executive with an extensive background in clinical research, came to us as a result of an ongoing conflict. She and her boss, Beth, shared a history as former colleagues and had enjoyed a ten-year friendship outside of work. When Beth needed a new director to join her team, she encouraged Janet to apply for the position. Although Janet had reservations about working for a friend, she respected Beth and applied for the role with enthusiasm.

Once hired, she recognized that she and Beth had significantly different leadership approaches and styles. As time passed, their differences grew more obvious and pronounced. Janet strongly disagreed with Beth's management decisions in several key areas but was convinced that voicing her concerns to Beth would backfire. Staff members expressed frustration and confusion about the mixed messages they were receiving from their department's two leaders. Janet, reluctant to confront Beth for fear of jeopardizing their friendship, found herself in a perpetual state of reactivity. Coiled like a spring much of the time at work, she felt herself ready to snap at the slightest provocation.

When we began working together, Janet was preparing to launch a job search for a new position, convinced that the only solution to her conflict at work was to leave her position altogether. She reached out for coaching in the hope that she could discover her "voice" in her working relationship with Beth while still preserving their friendship, which she cherished. If she could find a way to honor her own expertise and leadership instincts while still respecting Beth's role and authority, she might be able to continue in her position, reduce her stress level, and maintain their friendship.

In our first sessions together, Janet described the impact this conflict had on her physical well-being. She carried her anxiety and stress in her shoulders and upper back. She arrived home after work exhausted and depleted. We noticed a tremulous quality to her voice, as if the experience of holding back from expressing herself at work had compromised her vocal strength and volume.

Janet expressed a sincere interest and openness to adopting new practices into her routine that would reconnect her to her resilience and inner strength and reduce her anxiety at work.

We suggested that Janet incorporate a physical practice into her routine that we refer to as Centering (see page 214 in the appendix for a full description of the Centering practice). She learned to tune into her body, notice where she was holding tension, and relax those muscles in her body that were contracted. As she relaxed, she was able to project a calmer presence. As her belly softened, she was able to breathe more deeply from her diaphragm and fill her lungs with more oxygen, which settled her nervous system's instinctive fight–flight instinct.

Once introduced to the practice of Centering, Janet used it enthusiastically throughout the day to self-manage when she found herself triggered. She even wore a ring she'd not worn in years as an intentional reminder to herself to Center periodically during the day so that she could recover more easily when she was triggered. As a result of her consistent practice, she observed that she entered into conversations with Beth and others at work from a more grounded and balanced place. Connecting with her physical center and reminding herself of what mattered most to her each day also enabled her to access her courage. She was able to have more thoughtful and direct conversations with Beth about their relationship and differences.

Though Janet landed on and committed to a variety of practices that helped her access her core strengths and take more assertive stands for herself, it was the ongoing practice of Centering that best aligned Janet with her leadership potential. As a result of her dedication to this new practice, Janet shaped herself to respond differently in triggering situations and cultivated a capacity for calm that opened up new possibilities for her in all of her relationships.

Your Turn

Reflecting on coping strategies that have helped you recover successfully when you're triggered is key to intentionally cultivating a capacity for calm and resilience. When you introduce new strategies or practices for returning yourself to your Center when you're provoked, you'll regain your equilibrium with even greater ease.

1. Recall a recent incident when you found yourself triggered but were able to recover and regain your balance rather quickly. What message did you give yourself that helped you return to Center? What action did you take that supported your recovery?

2. Reflect on the types of activities or practices that calm your mind and body. What are they? Pick one activity (from the inserted list of suggestions) or add one of your own to introduce and practice once a day for the next week and notice its impact on how well and easily you recover when triggered.

   - ☐ Take a break every few hours and get a breath of fresh air.
   - ☐ Do some gentle stretching periodically throughout the day.
   - ☐ At the end of the day, journal about the positive experiences you had that day.
   - ☐ Have a meal and/or visit with someone who routinely lifts your spirits.
   - ☐ Listen to music.
   - ☐ Practice some form of sitting or walking meditation.
   - ☐ Identify a physical location that soothes you and spend a few minutes in that location.

In his book *You Are Not Your Brain,* Schwartz and his colleague Dr. Rebecca Gladding suggest that, through intentional training and practice, you can reshape your tendencies by creating new neural pathways that enable your brain to choose different responses when you're triggered. The key is to become a trained observer of yourself and your thinking.

How can you hone this skill of paying attention to your thoughts without getting carried away by them? In his book *The Emotional Life of Your Brain,* Dr. Richard Davidson makes a compelling case for engaging in the tradition of sitting meditation, an ancient practice for cultivating resilience and calm.[5] Davidson, a professor of psychiatry and psychology at the University of Wisconsin at Madison, has proven the impact of meditation on reducing the negative emotions and distress that are triggered in the amygdala, part of the limbic system in the brain. Given the results of recent brain research that highlights neuroplasticity, or the ability the brain has to change and develop, it's now proven that mindfulness meditation establishes new neural connections between the prefrontal cortex and the amygdala, increasing the possibility of responding thoughtfully to triggers. The modern world of brain science has demonstrated the efficacy of a practice that Tibetan monks and other nonreligious meditation practitioners have embraced for centuries.

If you're not convinced that mindfulness meditation is for you, then finding another practice that invites you to focus and increases your sense of calm is another viable method for reducing your reactivity as a leader. We worked recently with a leader who found she couldn't commit wholeheartedly to a sitting meditation practice. She was, however, resolute in her commitment to face the chaos of her organization with composure and calm. In our work together, she landed on the practice of taking several five-minute pauses during the day and focusing her attention on her breath. She soon discovered that even the simple routine of focusing on her breath calmed her and enabled her to respond to stressful situations with less anxiety and reactivity.

Take a moment now to focus your attention on your breath. Let your shoulders drop back and relax, and allow your abdominal muscles to release. As you breathe from your diaphragm, follow your breath as it moves in and out of your nasal passages. Notice what's happening in your body right now. What's the quality of your presence? Imagine the potential positive impact of taking a pause to breathe deeply several times a day. Once you get into the habit of breathing deeply and accessing more oxygen routinely, it's more likely you'll be able to call on this habit when you need it most.

When you intentionally practice certain physical activities, such as Centering, mindfulness meditation, or deep breathing, you are actively building your body's ability to be grounded, open, and connected to the world around you. Routinely engaging in physical practices that are designed to cultivate this capacity means that when you are triggered by circumstances, your body knows how to respond skillfully.

Landing on new habits that support you in managing your own anxiety is imperative. Your natural instincts for fight, flight, freeze, or appease when your nervous system warns you of a valid threat serve you well. Your triggers, however, often masquerade as threats and provoke responses that are damaging rather than useful.

The Triggers Conversation and our recommended coaching actions and practices are designed to support you as you increase your awareness of your triggers and your conditioned responses. Equipped with greater self-awareness, you can introduce new habitual responses that you develop through intentional and mindful practice. You and the organization you lead will benefit from the calm and centered presence that you cultivate.

The Triggers Conversation: Key Takeaways

When you entered into the Triggers Conversation, we invited you to reflect on the nature of your triggers, how you tend to respond when triggered, and what helps you regain your center when you're in the grip of reactivity. Equipped with increased self-awareness and new practices, you are now better positioned to consciously choose your responses and regain your balance more easily when provoked. As Stephen Covey writes in his preface to the book, *Prisoners of Our Thoughts*, "between stimulus and response, there is a space. In that space is our power to choose our response. In our response lies our growth and freedom."[6] Your resilience as a leader depends on your ability to manage your responses to triggers with insight and skill.

The Triggers Conversation: What's Next?

Coaching Assignments for Leveraging Your Learning

Is the Triggers Conversation particularly critical for you? The following list of Actions, Practices, and Resources is a tool kit for engaging more deeply in this important Missing Conversation.

Action Steps

- Select a colleague or friend who embodies calm and resilience. Intentionally notice on a regular basis how she handles herself in tense situations, paying particular attention to her observable behaviors. Make efforts to model these behaviors yourself in difficult situations.
- Keep a Triggers Log (see page 216 in the appendix) for yourself: track on a daily basis who or what situations evoke a strong negative emotional response in you. Note not only the triggering event or person but also the physical sensations associated with being triggered and the actions you took in response. After two weeks, review your log and determine what you've learned about yourself and your triggers. Examine all of your examples for patterns or connections. What do these connections or patterns reveal about your triggers and how you tend to respond when triggered? Do you avoid the triggering situation? Do you blow up and confront? Shut down? Make nice? Reflect on how you can connect this learning to your leadership.

Ongoing Practices

- Centering can be a powerful practice for habitually grounding and aligning yourself with what matters most to you. See page 214 in the appendix for a detailed description of this practice.
- Pause for at least a minute several times a day over the next two weeks to engage in a practice of deep breathing. Rather than breathing from your upper chest, allow that area of your body to consciously relax. Imagine your breath dropping and settling into your diaphragm. Breathe from that part of your body. Extend your exhale so that you breathe out all the air from your lungs. Your next inhale will be much deeper and engage more of your full lung capacity. Through routine practice, you'll breathe more deeply generally, which will help you maintain your calm when you're provoked.
- Over the next two weeks, introduce a practice of pausing for five minutes three times a day simply to notice your thoughts, feelings,

and physical sensations. Stepping into your observer mode to notice your experience will help you to recognize the early warning signs of reactivity.

Suggested Resources

Emotions Revealed: Recognizing Faces and Feelings to Improve Communication and Emotional Life by Paul Ekman: St. Martin's Press, 2003.

The Leadership Dojo: Build Your Foundation as an Exemplary Leader by Richard Strozzi-Heckler: Frog, 2007.

Search Inside Yourself: The Unexpected Path to Achieving Success, Happiness (and World Peace) by Chade-Meng Tang: HarperCollins, 2012.

PART II

Conversations That Boost Satisfaction

I don't think that there are any limits to how
excellent we could make life seem.

—**Jonathan Safran Foer,**
Everything Is Illuminated

How satisfied are you with your leadership experience right now? If we took a series of snapshots of you throughout your day, how often would we catch you smiling?

The nervous system is designed to maximize pleasure and minimize pain. If humans are hardwired to seek satisfaction, why is it then that so many leaders we meet feel dissatisfied in their role and seek out coaching for relief?

Do you share their frustration? Do you yearn to feel more joy in your leadership but struggle to move past habits that keep greater satisfaction just out of your reach? Do you believe that the only way to be a true leader is to sacrifice yourself—along with your happiness?

The good news: you can be a masterful leader and take care of yourself. In fact, when you bring your mindful attention to the three conversations in our next section, you'll discover strategies and practices that both strengthen your effectiveness and increase your fulfillment. Our clients have taught us that the reflections that matter most to a leader's contentment and vitality focus on three key areas. The Capacity, Well-Being, and Career Crossroads Conversations invite you to enter into these reflections and create an opening for more choice, balance, and joy.

CHAPTER 4

How Much Is Enough? The Capacity Conversation

Overcommitting will eventually erode your identity or your life.

—**Bob Dunham**, *The Innovator's Way*

The *Macmillan Dictionary* defines *capacity* as "the amount of work or goods that a company or person can produce."[1] According to the *Business Dictionary, capacity* is "the specific ability of an entity (person or organization) or resource, measured in quantity and level of quality, over an extended period."[2] Google defines *capacity* as "the maximum amount that something can contain" or "fully occupying the available space."[3]

Two things are clear from these definitions. First, capacity is a function of several factors, including time, space, resources, and abilities. And second, while you might not like to admit it, your capacity is not infinite. Although you can expand your capacity by improving your skills, adding resources, or developing better energy renewal habits (which we'll explore in the next chapter), at any one point in time, your capacity is what it is—you have a "maximum amount" of commitments on which you can effectively deliver. Beyond that, you are overcommitted.

One evening as we were taking a break from writing this book, we saw an AT&T commercial that played repeatedly during prime-time television. Its core message says a lot about why so many of us end up overcommitted at work on a regular basis.

The commercial features an adult man, dressed in a business suit, sitting at a small table with a group of kindergartners in a classroom. "Who thinks more is better?" he asks. All of the kids raise their hands. "OK, why?" he asks one young girl. "Why is more better?"

"Because sometimes your parents don't let you have more because there's not enough, and like, you really like it and you want more," she responds excitedly, her voice going up an octave. "WE WANT MORE!" she shouts. "WE WANT MORE!" She leaps up from the table and jumps up and down while the other children nod in agreement.

At this point the picture fades to a map of the United States that shows the breadth of AT&T's 4G network, followed by an authoritative voice-over declaring, "It's not complicated. *More is better.*" Although that message may be good for AT&T, it reflects a deep and unquestioned assumption that may be driving your behavior at work, sometimes in ways that don't serve you well.

More is better, or so you are often told: more work, wealth, growth, profits, success, and possessions. Many people are often in the pursuit of more. But why? Is more *always* better?

When it comes to managing your capacity, the answer is no. What is capacity management? It is the ability to make and manage your commitments *in a way that satisfies your customers, is sustainable over time, and allows you to take care of your whole life.* In other words, you are able to produce satisfaction without creating burnout. To manage your capacity well, you must know where the line is between saying yes to enough opportunities to grow and sustain your career and your organization and taking on too much. Until you ask yourself the key question posed in this chapter—how much is enough?—you can't know when you've crossed that line. In fact, you might not even see that there *is* a line! With your vision blurred, it's all too easy to overcommit.

And when you overcommit, the results don't just impact you—they impact your team and organization, too. Organizations that are chronically overcommitted are not effective or successful in the long run. Despite the best efforts of their employees, they don't consistently fulfill their commitments on time and as promised. If they do, fulfillment often comes at the sacrifice of their employees' health and well-being. Overcommitted teams and organizations experience breakdowns in trust with key stakeholders, lose credibility in the eyes of others, and suffer low employee morale and burnout. Ultimately, they jeopardize their mission and their future.

Just how pervasive is this problem of overcommitment? The Families and Work Institute conducted a comprehensive study of American workers that revealed that one in three employees report being chronically overworked.[4] A subsequent study reported that the more overworked employees are, the more likely they are to:

- Make mistakes at work
- Feel angry at their employer for expecting so much
- Resent their coworkers who don't work as hard
- Experience greater levels of stress, poorer health, and higher levels of depression

The solution to the dilemma is to manage your capacity and the capacity of your organization. More good news: capacity management is a learnable skill that allows you to prevent overcommitment when you can and to deal more effectively with it when you can't. That said, many leaders have not been taught how to manage their capacity well or how to manage the capacity of their teams and organizations. This certainly was the case for the three leaders you'll meet later in this chapter. Their capacity management struggles may mirror your own challenges and provide you with new insights for managing them.

As is the case with many of the Missing Conversations outlined in this book, engaging in the Capacity Conversation takes courage: the courage to face your fears, which are at the heart of why you overcommit in the first place. Some people fear the prospect of not being enough or of disappointing others; other people fear admitting limitations or failing outright. As you begin this conversation, we invite you to face your fears head-on. On the other side of your fear is a newfound freedom from the never-ending cycle of too much to do and too little time, along with a renewed sense of hope and possibility about the future.

PHASE 1: UNEARTH YOUR TENDENCIES TO OVERCOMMIT

The number one rule of effective capacity management is this: only say yes to those commitments that you have the time, energy, and resources to fulfill. This may seem like common sense, but it is a rule that many people and organizations break on a regular basis.

Of course, we've all been overcommitted on occasion—and sometimes, as a short-term strategy, taking on too much makes sense. For example, you might say yes to a last-minute request from an important client even though your plate is already full, because you believe it will secure the relationship and potentially lead to additional business. To fulfill the request, you work the entire weekend, cancel your other commitments, and forgo some sleep. When you deliver the product Monday morning to rave reviews, you're delighted. So is your client—and your boss. Sound familiar?

What could be wrong with this picture? You've satisfied your customer and yourself. However, you'll recall that capacity management is about making and managing your commitments in a way that is both satisfying *and* sustainable. If working through the weekend to fulfill client demands becomes the only strategy you have for managing an ever-expanding number of commitments and deliverables, you're risking burnout, failure to deliver—or both.

The point here is that there's a big difference between being overcommitted on occasion and being *chronically* overcommitted. Chronic overcommitment is when you *regularly* have more commitments on your plate than you have the time, energy, or resources to deliver on, and you feel like *there is no end in sight*—as if you are running full speed on a treadmill with no way of getting off and no chance of slowing down.

The costs of being chronically overcommitted are significant. In this chapter, our focus will be on the impact overcommitment has on your ability to deliver results and maintain your reputation as a trustworthy and reliable performer. But overcommitment takes a huge toll on your well-being and health, something we address more deeply in chapter 5.

Take a moment to look at the following signs of chronic overcommitment. How many of these signs do you see in yourself? How many of these do you see in those you lead?

The Signs of Chronic Overcommitment

- You feel anxious about your ability to deliver on key commitments, and you wonder how you'll pull it off. This pushes you into a never-ending cycle of working longer and harder to achieve results.
- You're frequently late to meetings or reschedule them.
- A frenetic pace characterizes your days.
- You're experiencing breakdowns in other parts of your life: family, health, key relationships, and so on.
- You're dropping balls either personally or professionally.
- You're feeling increasingly resentful of the pace and volume of your work.

Given the extraordinary toll that overcommitting takes, why does anyone do it? The truth is, many organizations are actually built on a strategy of overcommitting to customers. They count on being able to figure out later how they'll deliver. Sometimes they pull it off; sometimes they don't. And many leaders today feel tremendous pressure to say yes to every request made of them, whether they have the capacity to fulfill them or not.

The external pressures that cause people to overcommit are sometimes easier to see, and often become the focal point of blame. You have to overcommit, you might say to yourself or to others, because your corporate culture, your boss, or your marketplace demands that you do. Although it's true that these external forces can exert enormous pressure, in the end, the place of true leverage and change is within you. You are the *only* person who can transform your life from overcommitted to fully committed—and the Capacity Conversation is essential to that radical and powerful change.

Finding the Line: Rob's Story

Some of our clients have built their careers on saying yes and doing more—with disastrous consequences for their personal lives. Our client, Rob, was a rising star in his company—but at what cost?

Before we ever met him, we heard a great deal about Rob from some of his colleagues in the fast-paced entrepreneurial company where he worked. We'd been hired to prepare a group of leaders, including Rob, for the expanded roles and responsibilities they were expected to assume as the company grew. He was somewhat new to the company, but he had already made a mark; the CEO had singled him out and told him, "I wish I had ten other directors like you." Rob was racking up an impressive track record of results: expanding business, winning over disgruntled clients, and successfully managing the company's largest accounts.

However, the thing Rob was most known for among his peers was not his track record but rather his habit of sending e-mails at 3:00 A.M., his tendency to talk about the crazy travel schedule he kept, and his unbridled drive. When we finally met Rob for his first coaching session, it was clear that he was not managing his capacity effectively. He was late for his session, came in out of breath, spoke rapidly about the many deliverables for which he was responsible, and had a very hard time being present for our conversation. It was clear he didn't have the capacity for another commitment—including coaching—and we wondered if he would show up with enough presence and focus to benefit from our work with him.

Rob was late—again—for our second coaching session. He hadn't completed his prework, and he cut the session short to attend another meeting. Not wanting to waste his time or ours, we told Rob that he didn't appear to have the space in his schedule for coaching and suggested he opt out of the program. To our surprise, Rob was quite taken aback and insisted he wanted to continue. We agreed, but on the condition that he come prepared, committed, and ready to give his best.

Rob kept his next several sessions and was on time for each. We shared our assessment of his scattered and frenetic presence, along with his reputation as a hard-charging, ambitious colleague who worked around the clock. This was sobering to him. Once Rob paused long enough to think about it, he realized that he wanted to be known for his strategic thinking gifts, his ability to build and manage a team, and his skill in dealing with clients—not for the hours that he kept or the unrelenting pace that marked his days.

However, working hard, saying yes, and driving himself until he got results had helped Rob get to where he was. He could see that he was overcommitted, but he simply didn't know another way to work. And given his track record and support from the CEO, he wasn't sure he needed to discover one.

We pointed out that Rob was operating from the assumption that AT&T commercial had hammered home: more is better, no matter the cost. But Rob was beginning to see that his response to rising demand was actually eroding his contribution and impact. By his own admission, he was fatigued much of the time, wasn't thinking as clearly or crisply as he usually did, and wasn't using much of his creativity to generate new ideas and approaches for serving clients. For Rob, more wasn't better; rather, it was depleting him.

Rob felt responsible for helping others and didn't want to see them, or the company, fail. This noble impulse pushed Rob to tackle problems and worry about responsibilities that didn't fall under his oversight. We suggested to Rob that he observe this tendency in himself. We asked him to pause before he stepped in to offer assistance or said yes to someone's plea for help. Rob would be stuck on the overcommitment treadmill until he learned to concentrate on fulfilling those deliverables that were truly his to own and say no to those that weren't. He was on the verge of burnout—and if Rob went down, so would his team. Though his impulse was noble, he was actually failing his colleagues rather than supporting them.

The real turning point came when Rob spent a weekend home alone with his three small children while his wife was out of town. Because Rob regularly worked late, traveled constantly, and was gone from home three days out of every week, he had lost touch with his family. This became painfully clear over the weekend when he realized he didn't really know his kids or appreciate the role his wife played as a single parent much of the time. Being home alone with his children showed him just how distant he had grown from them. This gave him a newfound resolve to manage his capacity differently.

The first change Rob made was to draw a boundary around his daily work schedule by leaving the office by 6:30 or 7 P.M. most evenings and by going offline by 10:00 P.M. every night. (No more 3:00 A.M. e-mails!) He also cut travel to twice a month, on average, instead of every week. This was a difficult change to make. Rob traveled as much as he did because he enjoyed the face time with clients. He thrived on the praise he heard regularly, such as, "We could really use you at the next meeting, Rob. No one knows how to calm the client down like you do." Rob's colleagues pushed back at first when he cut down his travel, and a few times he caved to their demands. Over time, however, he held his ground. Soon, he was able to spend more time home with his family.

In our coaching sessions, Rob came to realize that he needed help if he was to successfully manage the complexity and breadth of his client engagements. He requested one new person for his team—someone from another group in the company that he knew could come on board and make a contribution right away. At first his boss pushed back. After all, Rob had done so well without the extra help, and resources were tight. But Rob insisted that additional human resources were essential to the continued growth and success of his client engagements, and his manager eventually relented. Given that he had a solid track record and was respected widely for the results he'd achieved, Rob was able to negotiate from a place of strength.

Rob continued to work hard and to drive results—he enjoyed his work and he wanted to continue to grow his career and help the company succeed. But engaging in the Capacity Conversation had shown him the clear line between working well and working over capacity. He was able to manage his schedule and his commitments more effectively. This in turn helped him to be more effective in his leadership role, while allowing him to attend to his roles as father and husband. Later that year, Rob was promoted to VP. Over time, his reputation also changed, from the consummate road warrior who never slept to a strong, creative problem solver and leader.

Your Turn

Take a few minutes to reflect on your own capacity management challenges and to identify some initial steps you might take to begin managing your capacity more effectively.

1. Are you experiencing breakdowns in satisfying your customers, either external or internal? In sustaining your leadership efforts over time? In your ability to take care of the other important facets of your life, such as your family or your health? How ready and willing are you to change this?

2. What are the three reasons you are most likely to overcommit? Take a look below at the reasons for overcommitting that we've listed and identify the ones that are your key drivers.

3. What is one small step you could take today to begin managing your capacity more effectively?

Common Reasons for Overcommitment

Here are some of the underlying reasons why you may find yourself on the overcommitment treadmill. You'll notice that some of them have to do with your environment, some are related to what you value or fear, and others are based on untested assumptions. Which of these are true for you?

1. *I struggle with saying no.* I don't know how to say no without offending someone, or I haven't granted myself the permission to say no, especially to those who have authority over me.

2. *I'm afraid of the consequences.* I have a story about dire consequences that I'll incur if I do push back. I assume I'll be demoted, fired, or passed by for promotion. I haven't tested these assumptions; I treat them as facts.
3. *I like to help people.* When I'm asked to do so, especially on the spot, my default is to say yes, regardless of whether I have the capacity.
4. *I'm good at what I do.* People know it, and they frequently ask for my help. It feeds my ego when they ask (who doesn't like to be needed and wanted, after all?) and so I say yes—even when my plate is already full.
5. *I am part of a workplace culture that chronically overcommits.* I've chosen to be a product and enforcer of this culture rather than a leader who seeks to change it.
6. *I want to prove my worth.* I'm in a new role or leading a new team and I want to prove my value to potential customers.
7. *I'm a high achiever and I thrive on challenge, growth, and change.* I've made a career out of doing more and achieving more than others. Unfortunately, I've never learned where the line is between a lot of work and too much work.
8. *My strengths lead me to overcommit.* I assume I will always rise to the challenge of taking on more—until I don't.
9. *I equate* doing *more with* being *more.* If I'm not doing more, I don't know how else to define the value I add.

Now that you can see more clearly why you overcommit and what it costs you when you do, let's turn our attention to how you get off the overcommitment treadmill. But before we do, remember the power that can come from taking one small step in the right direction.

This certainly was true for another one of our clients. Her boss, like Rob, regularly sent e-mails late at night, and she felt compelled to respond—but feeling as though her workday never ended left her exhausted and resentful. Her initial step toward better capacity management was to give herself the permission to stop checking her e-mail after 8:00 P.M. This small change ended up making a huge difference in how she felt about her life. It meant there was an actual end to her workday. She could "lay her burdens down" and pick them back up with greater effectiveness and ease the next morning. While she couldn't stop her boss from sending e-mails after 8:00 P.M., she could decide for herself when she would respond and then manage her boss's expectations accordingly.

Phase 2: Align Your Commitments with Your Capacity

Once we come to the conclusion that we're overcommitted, what can we do to rebalance our lives—and how do we prevent overcommitment from happening again? This phase of the Capacity Conversation asks you to explore a three-step process for aligning your commitments with your capacity:

1. *Declare a breakdown.* Acknowledge your overcommitment and take ownership for resolving it.
2. *Initiate a Capacity Management Assessment.* We'll show you how to take a thorough inventory of all of your commitments, make an assessment as to which ones you may not have the capacity to fulfill, and a devise a game plan for addressing them.
3. *Communicate with your stakeholders.* Initiate conversations with your customers, your boss, and other key stakeholders that may be impacted by your current capacity management challenges. Gain their support and partnership as you take the next steps.

The Capacity Conversation requires that you make an internal shift in the way you see yourself. Bob Dunham, the author we cited at the beginning of this chapter, calls this shift "accepting your finitude."[5] This is the foundation for effectively managing your capacity.

Accepting your finitude means acknowledging that you are not perfect, nor do you need to be. It means accepting that you are a human being with limitations and giving yourself permission to act in accordance with those limits. When you accept your finitude, you fully embrace the fact that you can't possibly know everything, do everything, or please everyone. And once you do, a new world of possibilities opens up.

Accepting your finitude is incredibly freeing. It frees you to set boundaries, gives you the resolve to say no more often, allows you to take the time to renew yourself without feeling guilty, and releases you from the never-ending belief that you are not enough. You only believe you are not enough when you hold yourself to an impossible standard of being infinite, all knowing, and without limits. In doing so, you set yourself up for repeated disappointment and feelings of failure when, despite your best efforts and hard work, you discover you're none of those things. Instead of pressing on and trying to conceal this fact, you can acknowledge it openly and honor it—a gift to yourself and to everyone with whom you live and work.

This certainly was true for our client Lea, who was blindsided by a breakdown in delivery from one of her best project managers. Thanks to the Capacity Conversation, she was able to bring her commitments and those of her team in line with their capacity.

From Frenzy to Ease: Lea's Story

As the VP for the largest division in her organization, Lea was a busy executive with a reputation for getting things done and being responsive to the doctors whom she and her association served. When we began working with her, she was dealing with several challenges, including managing difficult personalities on her team, being understaffed, and managing a huge and growing workload. Not surprisingly, she and her staff were stretched thin, and the stress and strain were beginning to show.

Lea had a tendency to say yes to the many requests that came her way without thinking of the resources her team needed or whether they had the capacity to fulfill those requests. Her staff wished she would push back more, but Lea got the message from her boss that she should say yes first and then figure out later how to fulfill the growing demand.

As we sat with Lea for her initial coaching session, we discussed the extent to which she felt overwhelmed and how she telegraphed this to her team. Lea admitted that just that morning she had been rushing frantically down the hall to a meeting. "I better put my roller blades on, it's going to be another one of those days!" she'd joked. As she reflected on this statement, she decided that though it might have been funny to her, it probably wasn't funny to her staff and most likely contributed to their anxiety.

Lea's first proactive step was to be more conscious of when she herself was overwhelmed. When she felt anxious about the many demands she was dealing with, she would take a deep breath, slow down, and release some of the tension she tended to store in her shoulders, neck, and jaw. This simple move helped her to calm down and think more clearly about the situation at hand. As she managed her own stress better, her team felt less pressured and overwhelmed as well.

One of Lea's best project managers was particularly stressed and overcommitted. She was a high achiever who pushed herself and her colleagues hard to deliver results and was known for getting things done that others couldn't seem to accomplish. However, she was starting to burn out, as evidenced by a breakdown in the delivery of an important project. Not wanting to admit that she couldn't handle everything on her plate, Lea's employee had opted instead to work around the clock, hoping she'd be able to pull it off. When she didn't, she blamed the demanding doctors, the lack of resources and support, and the other department with which she'd coordinated. The only person at whom she didn't point a finger was herself.

We suggested that Lea ask her employee to complete a Capacity Management Assessment. Lea sat down with her to figure out what she needed going forward to ensure she could be successful without burning herself out. Because Lea's entire team was carrying such a huge workload and had been chronically understaffed, Lea also asked her other direct reports to complete a Capacity Management Assessment and talk with her about how best to prioritize their work, fulfill the commitments they could, and renegotiate or defer those they couldn't. As a result of her team conversations, Lea was better prepared to talk to her boss about the additional resources they needed and how best to evaluate their competing priorities.

In light of her capacity management challenges, Lea decided her number one priority had to be hiring for the two additional positions she had yet to fill. In the meantime, she practiced pushing back and saying no when necessary. When a new request was made of her department, she would ask her boss if it was the organization's highest priority. If so, she got agreement on what other commitments they could defer to make room for it. Once she had the missing conversation with her boss about the priorities of the organization and the capacity of her department, her boss was more than willing to support her.

The biggest change for Lea came when she learned to accept the fact that she couldn't do it all. Her best was good enough: she didn't have to be Superwoman and exceed all expectations. Once she accepted this, Lea was free to manage her capacity, and the capacity of her department, in a new and much more effective way. Her direct reports were still stretched thin until new resources were added to the team, but they could see an end in sight. They also found hope in Lea's newfound resolve to do what was needed for them to succeed.

Your Turn

1. To what extent have you accepted your finitude? How might embracing and honoring your limits make you a more effective leader?

2. What is your Achilles' heel when it comes to pushing back? To whom do you struggle to say no even when you know saying yes isn't prudent? How might saying no or at least pushing back on some of the demands and requests you receive help you or your team?

3. We can expand our capacity by adding people, developing new skills, improving and streamlining key processes, and improving coordination and communication among team members. What steps might you need to take as a leader to expand your team or your organization's capacity?

4. In the preceding story, Lea conducted a Capacity Management Assessment and asked her team members to do the same. Take a look at the instructions for completing your own Capacity Management Assessment. To what extent might this be an important next step for you?

Conducting a Capacity Management Assessment

A Capacity Management Assessment includes an inventory of all of your commitments, an assessment as to which ones you may not have the capacity to fulfill, and a game plan for addressing the situation. The Capacity Management Assessment is a great tool for your team as well.

1. *List all your commitments*, including all projects, responsibilities, and deliverables that are currently on your plate. Rank them in order of priority.
2. *Identify the red flags.*[5] Which commitments are in danger of not being fulfilled on time or as expected without adding resources, reprioritizing, or taking other commitments off your plate?
3. *Triage.* The options available to you for each red flag include the following: Defer, Delegate, Transfer, Decline, or Renegotiate. The choices you make must be based on a clear understanding of the priorities of your organization, the needs of your customers, and the desires of your internal stakeholders.

If you lead a team of people and you are not sure they have the capacity to fulfill their commitments, we suggest you ask them to complete a Capacity Management Assessment. Then engage in a conversation with each of them about how best to move forward to satisfy their customers, prevent breakdowns, or take care of any that may have already occurred.

The Art of Saying No

Overcommitment means you don't have the capacity for one more project, task, or deliverable. Inevitably, you will have to decline some requests while you work to expand capacity or rearrange priorities. But how do you say no to clients, your boss, or other stakeholders who are accustomed to hearing you say yes without eroding their confidence in you?

First, develop a solid track record of consistently delivering on your commitments, which will build your identity as a trustworthy and reliable performer. Then, when and if you need to decline, you can do so from a place of strength and legitimacy.

Second, when you decline a request, express your answer from a place of genuine commitment to serving your customer, your boss, or your stakeholder better. If you are truly committed to providing excellent results, you know that overcommitting is not the way to get the job done. You're declining because you are committed to satisfaction, meeting expectations, and delivering great work—three goals you can't achieve if you're overcommitted.

In the next part of this chapter, we explore other legitimate responses to requests besides saying yes. Expanding your ability to use these other options will buy you time and enable you to decline with greater resolve if you decide that is the right move to make.

PHASE 3: MAKE COMMITMENTS MATTER

As you have seen in the stories that we've shared so far, capacity management doesn't happen in isolation. As you strive to manage your own capacity more effectively, you can be frustrated and derailed by your colleagues' decisions and actions. For example, do they fulfill their own commitments? Produce quality work? Have the ability to push back appropriately with customers and stakeholders? The answers to those questions can make a big difference in your own capacity management efforts.

For that reason, it is all the more important to build rigor into the way you make and manage your commitments and coordinate work with others. When you do, you are able to influence the quality, quantity, and timeliness of the results you achieve with and through others.

We have found that four essential ingredients can make this coordination flow smoothly:

- Make effective requests
- Gain commitment
- Respond to requests thoughtfully
- Make productive complaints

Let's explore each of these four ingredients and see how they can help in your quest to manage your capacity more effectively.

1. Make Effective Requests

The cycle of coordinating work begins when you make a request or others make a request of you. This is a defining moment in your day. Whenever you make or respond to a request, you are creating a certain kind of future for yourself and others. How well you make requests can have a significant impact on your results.

Unfortunately, many people issue requests without much thought or care as to how they are framed or how other people will respond. In the busy and frenetic pace of organizational life, you can fall into the habit of issuing requests as if you are delivering newspapers: throwing them out quickly, while you are on the run, without much dialogue and without knowing for certain whether your request was received.

This violates the cardinal rule of requests: making a request is about gaining genuine commitment to get something done that matters. Many people are simply looking for a yes and don't pay attention to whether the commitment that they've received is something in which they can be confident.

This is a crucial distinction. As we've said earlier in this chapter, many people feel pressure to say yes to all the requests made of them, especially those that come from their bosses or their customers. If yes is the only acceptable answer, it doesn't mean very much.

The person who has said yes to your request may in fact not understand the request, not have the capacity to fulfill it, or not know how to. If any of these are true, you will likely have a breakdown in delivery—costing you time, money, and satisfaction.

Effective requests get impressive results. The next time you make a request, be sure you take the time to:

- Make a connection with the person on the other end of your request.
- Be clear about what you want, why it matters, and when you need it (and "ASAP" doesn't count!).
- Pay attention to the level of clarity and commitment that you are generating in the conversation; if you have any doubts about the other person's understanding of your request or his capacity to fulfill it, ask, don't assume.

These simple steps will get you to a yes you can count on.

2. Gain Commitment

A commitment is *a shared understanding of who will do what, by when, that a performer owns.* Your ability to get results and satisfy your customers is based on the quality of your commitments. If there isn't shared understanding of what needs to be done, clarity around who will do it, and a clear time frame for completing it, you can be sure of one thing: a breakdown in delivery.

3. Respond to Requests Thoughtfully

Responding thoughtfully and with integrity requires that you expand the range of responses that you can *skillfully give to a requestor,* along with the number of responses *you are willing to hear* from others. Following are six legitimate responses to requests:

- *Seek clarification.* "I'm not sure what your expectations are around the content of the report. Can you tell me more about what you want it to look like and when you need to have it?"

- *Accept the request.* "Yes, I commit to doing X by Y."
- *Counteroffer.* "I can't do X by Y, but here is what I can do. Will that work for you?"
- *Commit-to-commit.* "I need to check with my team before I commit. I'll get back to you with a firm answer by noon tomorrow."
- *Conditional commitment.* "I can do X by Y if __________ happens."
- *Decline.* "I am not able to commit to that. Here's why."

Before deciding which of these is best for a given situation, it's useful to get into the habit of pausing before you respond and asking yourself a few questions:

- Am I clear about what the other person is expecting and asking of me?
- Do I have the capacity to deliver as requested? How do I know?
- How will this impact my ability to deliver on other commitments?
- Am I willing to be held accountable for anticipating potential problems and breakdowns?

Ensure your own commitments are as meaningful as the commitments you ask of others; a reputation for keeping your word will encourage your colleagues to do the same.

4. Make Productive Complaints

There's a big difference between *complaining* and *making a productive complaint.* Complaining is a way of venting but usually does nothing to correct or improve a situation. A productive complaint is what you do when you *talk to the right person at the right time, from the right frame of mind, about a breakdown in a commitment the person made to you.* Perhaps the person missed a deadline, didn't meet your standards in the work he delivered, or failed to manage your expectations.

A productive complaint should only be made when there was a clear commitment in place; otherwise, you may be trying to hold someone accountable for something that she didn't know, understand, or agree to do.

Making a productive complaint can help you feel less resentful, provide an opportunity for new agreements to be made, and enable you to prevent future breakdowns. Without this important capacity management ingredient, you may end up correcting the work of others without giving them feedback on what went wrong, avoiding certain people whom you assess as not up to the task, or venting your frustrations to the wrong people.

Our client Ken didn't have the four essential ingredients of effective commitments at his disposal. As you read about his capacity management challenges, notice what resonates for you.

Making New Moves: Ken's Story

Ken was a trained physician, a seasoned manager in a pharmaceutical company, and an accomplished artist. Smart, capable, and possessed of unusual stamina, Ken was drowning in a sea of never-ending requests, deliverables, and projects. His organization had been understaffed and overcommitted for more than a year. Many of the employees with whom he worked faced the same challenge he did: despite their best efforts, they couldn't seem to get on top of their workload.

Not surprisingly, Ken's boss was also stretched thin and bombarded by constant challenges, changes, and emergencies that demanded her immediate attention. She drove Ken and her other staff as hard as possible to deliver on what seemed to them to be unreasonable requests and deadlines. Just when Ken felt as if he was getting a handle on his workload and priorities, his boss would throw another curveball at him and make it clear that she expected him to handle it. Ken, in turn, would push his own staff just as hard.

When we began working with Ken as part of a company-wide leadership development program, it was clear that he was overcommitted. To keep up with the constant demands of his job, he had quit a part-time volunteer job that he loved, abandoned his home improvement project to work weekends, and stopped taking time for lunch. Not only that, there were many commitments on his plate that were past due, in limbo, or in danger of not being fulfilled. This was a terrible burden for Ken, who prided himself on doing good work and moving things along.

We shared with Ken the four essential ingredients of making and managing commitments and concentrated on helping him to expand his repertoire of responses to his boss's incessant requests. Ken believed that you did what your boss asked you to do, regardless of whether it made sense. His only response to her requests were "yes" or "we'll do our best." Declining was a huge challenge for him, so we encouraged him to incorporate counteroffers and commit-to-commits. Whenever his boss caught him off guard with yet another request, he told her he needed to check first with his team and to consider the other commitments on his plate and then promised to get back to her later that day with a thoughtful answer that she could count on.

We also suggested that Ken pay more attention to how he made requests of his team and to notice whether he had a clear commitment at the end of every conversation. If not, his job was to ask questions and determine what his team needed to be able to deliver as requested.

Over time, Ken became more skillful in pushing back on his boss's requests when he felt they were unclear, unreasonable, or beyond his capacity to fulfill. His boss responded in a fair and reasonable way, and over time, this repaired some of the trust that had eroded between them. He also got better at gaining true commitment from his own team and grew more confident in their ability to deliver. Ken's capacity management efforts enabled him to establish some much-needed breathing room in his day. He even managed to take back his lunch.

Your Turn

1. Take a look again at the six responses to requests that we identified on page 90. Which of these responses do you use now? Which ones don't you use, and how does this impact you and your team? Pick one that you want to use more often and resolve to practice it this week.

2. How effective are you at making clear requests and gaining genuine commitment from your team? What might you do to improve?

3. Has a colleague or employee of yours missed an important deadline, not met your expectations, or failed to deliver on a key commitment? Consider making a productive complaint if you haven't already done so.

Ken eroded his reputation as a reliable and trustworthy performer with his tendency to give and accept what we call "sloppy promises." A sloppy promise (e.g., "I'll try my best" or "I'll see what I can do") is one that has an "escape clause" you can call on if you aren't able to fulfill as requested. Sloppy promises happen when you aren't confident in your ability to deliver but don't know how to decline, counteroffer, or use a commit-to-commit to determine your actual capacity.

As you continue to engage in new ways of managing your capacity, listen for sloppy promises and help people to respond with a clearer, more grounded commitment instead. This simple yet important shift in how you coordinate work, along with the other tools and practices we've outlined in this chapter, will go a long way toward getting you and your team off the overcommitment treadmill.

THE CAPACITY CONVERSATION: KEY TAKEAWAYS

You've come to this chapter because you feel overwhelmed and overcommitted on a regular basis. You work harder and longer in an effort to dig yourself out, only to find yourself slipping back into overwhelm despite your best efforts. The only way out of this predicament is to engage rigorously and often in the Capacity Conversation.

This conversation began with a self-assessment to determine whether you are overcommitted, what it is costing you if you are, and what your choices are for moving forward. We invited you to take an unflinching look at the tendencies that fuel your overcommitment: the hidden, often unconscious reasons why you take on more than you can deliver.

Next, you learned how to build greater rigor into the way you coordinate work, including making effective requests, eliciting firm commitments and promises, responding to requests with integrity, and issuing productive complaints. As you continue to engage in the Capacity Conversation, you will expand your ability to satisfy your customers, sustain your leadership efforts over time, and attend to your whole life.

The Capacity Conversation: What's Next?

Coaching Assignments for Leveraging Your Learning

Is the Capacity Conversation particularly critical for you? The following list of Actions, Practices, and Resources is a tool kit for engaging more deeply in this important Missing Conversation.

Action Steps

- Make a Capacity Declaration.[6] This is an assessment of the number of hours you are willing and able to work, on average, each week and still take care of your whole life. For most managers and executives, this is somewhere between forty-five and fifty-five hours a week. Share your declaration with the important people in your life and enlist their support in helping you to keep it.
- Reflect on your direct reports and determine which of them may be struggling with overcommitment. Ask them to complete a Capacity Management Assessment and discuss the results with you.
- Assess the extent to which your organization as a whole is chronically overcommitted. If it is, engage with your peers and other leaders in the organization in a series of conversations to address its overcommitment systemically. Decide together what steps you might take collectively either to expand organizational capacity, decrease or defer current commitments and priorities, or both.

Ongoing Practices

- Become an observer of how you think and act when you are overwhelmed. Do you run worst-case scenarios through your head? Invent stories about the dire consequences you'll incur if you push back? Rush frantically through your day without pausing to notice the quality of your actions? Knowing how you operate when overwhelmed will help you catch yourself in this state and course correct as needed.

- When you find yourself overwhelmed, take a Six-Second Vacation.[7] This is from the book *The Anxious Organization* by Jeffrey Miller, and it's a proven practice for calming down and lessening anxiety. Here's how it works: inhale deeply for two seconds, sending much-needed oxygen to your muscles and brain, then exhale fully for two seconds, releasing stored tensions as you do. For the next two seconds, do nothing. Practice taking a Six-Second Vacation whenever you need to feel less overwhelmed.
- If declining requests is a struggle for you, make a commitment to say no or to decline one request each day to build your "no" muscle. Practice on an easy person to begin with, and build up to those people and situations that are most challenging for you.

Suggested Resources

The Anxious Organization: Why Smart Companies Do Dumb Things by Jeffrey Miller: Facts on Demand Press, 2008.

Conscious Business: How to Build Value through Values by Fred Kofman: Sounds True, 2006.

Who Will Do What by When: How to Improve Performance, Accountability and Trust with Integrity by Tom Hanson and Birgit Zacher Hanson: Heads-Up Performance, 2005.

CHAPTER 5

How Am I?
The Well-Being Conversation

The bigger our reservoir of value and well-being, the less emotionally vulnerable we are to the challenges we encounter every day.

—**Tony Schwartz,** *The Way We're Working Isn't Working*

In the introduction, we suggested that leadership is about calling forth others' best efforts as well your own. Sounds simple, doesn't it? But as you already know, this is much easier said than done. Exactly how do you access your best efforts and motivate others to do the same? Is there a proven process or formula you can follow to unlock the potential within you and those you lead?

Insight lies within reach when you consult your own experience for guidance. Consider for a moment the people in your life whom you admire most—mentors, friends, or family members. What traits do you cherish most in them? You may appreciate their intellect, respect their drive, or enjoy their sense of humor. But if you narrow your list down to those people whom you admire and who inspire you to be your best, the list probably shortens. These are the people who serve as a catalyst for your potential. In their presence, you feel capable of being and doing more.

If you're fortunate enough to have a person or two like this in your life, recall the last time you were with them. Try to remember your conversation and the way you felt about yourself. If you're like many of the clients with whom we work, you may notice that these role models have the ability to settle you while simultaneously igniting your desire to live and work more purposefully.

How do these people in your life manage to influence you in this way?

"Presence" is the answer. When you step back and consider your role models' impact on you, you'll undoubtedly identify the quality of their presence as the true source of their influence. In their company, you become more optimistic, energetic, and committed to action. Their well-being, the vitality and ease they embody, inspires you to call forth your best efforts. In essence, their wellness not only supports their best performance, it encourages your peak performance as well.

In chapter 2, we challenged you to reflect on the impact you most want to have on those you lead. We invited you to consider the influence of your mood on others and suggested that you intentionally cultivate the mood that will best support your desired impact. Here, in the Well-Being Conversation, we urge you to recognize the connection between your overall well-being, your presence, and your capacity to access your best efforts and encourage others to do the same.

Your well-being acts like a magnet for others' potential as well as your own. When you radiate wellness, you become a resource for those around you and more thoughtful and skillful in action. The question for leaders we coach is not whether their well-being matters but rather what being well really means for them. How can they successfully cultivate well-being in themselves and in others?

Being well means different things to different leaders. It may mean starting the day with excitement and energy or feeling more at peace about challenging circumstances. It could be as simple as walking up a flight of stairs without arriving breathless at the top. Some leaders we know characterize well-being as the capacity to be fully present and more joyful in their lives.

What does being well mean to you?

We define well-being as a sense of vitality in our body, mind, heart, and spirit. When we are well, we embody an ease and contentment that is observable to others. Your well-being includes, but extends beyond, the state of your physical health. As a leader, your wellness is reflected in your spirit and state of mind as much as it is in your physical health and fitness.

How would those around you characterize your well-being? What impressions are they forming of how content, at ease, and alive you are in your life and work? Just as your mood as a leader can be contagious by virtue of your position, the state of your well-being influences the well-being of others around you.

Your mind-set, your energy level, the emotions to which you have access, and the state of your physical health blend together to form the composite of your presence. When you give care and attention to these elements of your being, you are shaping yourself into a leader people move toward, listen to, and take guidance from.

How well you are is not just critical to your impact on others. It also directly influences your resilience. Today's increasingly complex environment demands that effective leaders bounce back from setbacks and embrace unanticipated change. Treating your wellness as a priority enables you to face challenges with greater resilience and less distress.

Though most people know this instinctively, they often move through work and life oblivious to the state of their health and vitality. We coach many leaders whose well-being suffers as a result of their drive to achieve results. Their dedication translates into self-sacrifice. This pattern is sustainable for a period of time, and some leaders have extraordinary stamina. But before long, many find they've lost their mojo. Their energy reserves are depleted. Some even face a health crisis that convinces them that this pattern of self-sacrifice comes at too great a cost.

When was the last time you assessed your physical, mental, emotional, and spiritual well-being? What's the cost to you, your team, and your organization if the state of your well-being continues to slip off your radar?

The clients whose stories we share in this chapter made a courageous choice to interrupt their cycle of self-sacrifice and examine the state of their health. In the process, they discovered that by making small adjustments, they could enhance their wellness and their positive impact on others. We invite you to do the same. In this chapter, you'll ask yourself, "How am I?" and listen carefully to yourself for an honest response.

PHASE 1: ASSESS YOUR VITALITY

Tackling the Well-Being Conversation can be daunting. It's like being lost in the wilderness without a compass or map. If you're like many of the clients with whom we work, exploring your state of well-being may feel like uncharted territory. You may even experience some initial internal resistance to turning your attention inward and assessing your wellness rather than focusing on your business or organizational goals.

But if you're resolved to prioritize your well-being, recognizing the current state of your well-being becomes essential to charting a clear path forward.

Like our client Valerie, whose story we share, you'll learn that acknowledging the current state of your vitality is essential to improving your overall wellness.

A Wake-Up Call for Action: Valerie's Story

Valerie sat down for our initial coaching intake session looking frazzled and distracted. A well-regarded and competent leader, she had recently been promoted to a senior management marketing role in her company and was eager to prove herself. As she opened a can of soda and a bag of chips to munch on, she described the pressures she found herself facing in her new, more demanding role. She had plotted her career path carefully, and her planning and focused determination had resulted in the promotion she'd been dreaming of. She'd reached out for coaching, though, because she'd been recently hospitalized for pneumonia and viewed this health scare as a wake-up call. She explained that the challenges of taking on expanded responsibilities at work while caring for aging parents and parenting twin boys had taxed her health and left her feeling generally depleted and discouraged.

Valerie explained that she'd missed a full week of work after her diagnosis and still didn't have the reserves of energy she felt she needed to manage all areas of her life. "If only," she explained, "I could find a way to boost my energy and feel enthusiastic again about my life and work. This role is what I've been hoping for and I don't want to screw it up! But if I slow down at all, I'm afraid I'll give executives the impression that I can't handle it. I know the pace I'm trying to maintain is draining me, but what options do I really have?"

Valerie acknowledged that something needed to change in the choices she was making and the schedule she was keeping. When we challenged her about her choice to say yes to this new position, she exclaimed with conviction that she was committed to being successful in this role. When we asked her about her duties as a daughter and a parent, she explained just as resolutely that being a responsive caretaker to her family was nonnegotiable.

Valerie wanted to perform better and feel more satisfied in all areas of her life. In our initial sessions, we proposed that the Well-Being Conversation was the critical step she needed to take to make inroads toward both agendas. Enhancing her wellness would give her the strength and energy to face the demands on her time without sacrificing herself in the process.

This revelation came as a surprise to Valerie, who admitted that she gave her well-being very little thought. When we asked Valerie what well-being meant to her, she shrugged and suggested that it mostly had to do with physical health. If she could get up in the morning and put in a long day, that translated to satisfactory well-being. We shared our Well-Being At-a-Glance Self-Assessment and suggested that her physical health, though critical, was only one of four essential elements of her overall wellness.

As we reviewed her assessment results together, she marveled that they felt so accurate. As if in Technicolor, she saw that her body and heart were suffering and accepted that these areas deserved her energy and attention.

Her only exercise involved walking to and from her car in the company parking lot and an occasional walk on the weekends with her children. Her eating habits had deteriorated and involved overeating late in the evening and skipping breakfast altogether. She recognized that anger and irritability were the emotions she felt most frequently. She couldn't remember the last time she'd felt joyful or calm.

With a handle on those areas of her well-being that demanded her attention most, Valerie discovered a renewed sense of direction and momentum. She identified some realistic and easy-to-implement adjustments and new habits that would meet these two areas of need. She found a yoga class to attend regularly that helped calm her mind and improve her flexibility and breathing. She agreed to stop eating lunch at her desk every day and give herself a few minutes to eat outdoors, have lunch with a colleague, or at least sit at the table in her office. She started to hold her one-on-one meetings with team members as walking meetings so she and each team member got some exercise and fresh air as they talked through important issues. She also introduced a practice of routinely noting what she was grateful for and found that her mood improved as a result.

Engaging in the Well-Being Conversation invited Valerie to create a practical set of action items that expanded her energy reserves—and her inner peace.

Your Turn

Complete the Well-Being At-a-Glance Self-Assessment. Tabulate your results for each area of your well-being and reflect on the following questions:

1. What do your results reveal about the areas of your well-being that most want your attention?
2. What impact do these areas of your well-being have on your leadership? On your personal life?

Well-Being At-a-Glance Self-Assessment

Instructions: Assess how true each statement is for you.
1 = Not true at all   2 = Rarely true   3 = Sometimes true
4 = Mostly true   5 = Always true

Your Body

____ I feel awake and rested most of the time.
____ My body is healthy, strong, and energetic.
____ I'm aware of what my body needs to operate at its best.
____ I pay attention to how I nourish my body.
____ I have the energy reserves I need to meet current and future challenges.

Your Mind

____ I experience peace of mind most of the time.
____ I'm able to be present in the moment for the person/people whom I am with.
____ I am alert and able to focus when it counts most.
____ I regularly greet the day with optimism and a sense of hopefulness.
____ I generally have more positive than negative thoughts about myself.

Your Heart

____ I experience positive emotions more frequently than negative emotions.
____ I am aware of what emotion I'm experiencing most of the time.
____ I'm able to express what I'm feeling to others.
____ I experience joy routinely in my life.
____ I'm usually compassionate toward others and myself.

Your Spirit

____ I experience a sense of purpose in my existence.
____ I find meaning and satisfaction in my work.
____ I know what matters most to me.
____ My daily choices align with what I value most in life.
____ I routinely notice beauty in the world around me.

In the end, you are the only person who can truly assess those areas of your well-being that are undernourished. Once you've identified them, you're ready to take the next step: letting go of the habits that are undermining your wellness.

PHASE 2: DETERMINE WHAT HABITS ARE NO LONGER SERVING YOU

You now know what areas of your well-being are clamoring for your attention, and you're ready to take action. If you're to put in place new habits and practices that will make a difference in the state of your body, heart, mind, and spirit, wouldn't it make sense to let go first of those habitual behaviors that sabotage you?

Like you, our client Glenn knew his habits needed an overhaul if he wanted to escape from a cycle of perpetual depletion. By engaging in phase 2 of the Well-Being Conversation, he made the changes that would alter his life.

When Resolve Dissolves the Status Quo: Glenn's Story

Glenn was deeply admired in his federal agency for his steadfast commitment to his office's mission and his technical expertise. His team members appreciated his approachability and commended him for his availability. He routinely pushed aside his own work to provide them coaching support.

Glenn stepped into our coaching engagement as part of a larger agency-wide leadership development initiative. He hoped coaching would help him build a more effective and capable team. Several conversations into our coaching relationship, Glenn mentioned his long work hours and his desire to control his weight with better discipline. As we dove deeper into these topics, the extent of Glenn's self-sacrifice emerged.

His typical day started a bit later than most of his colleagues' because he worked so late into the night. Arriving at the office by 9:30 A.M. most days, he'd move from meeting to meeting, providing team members with direction and support in between meetings when possible. He routinely worked until 8:00 or 9:00 P.M., munching on vending machine snacks when he felt hungry. If he could mobilize his energy, he might stop by the gym for a quick workout before heading home for a late dinner in front of the television. Exhausted by 11:00 P.M., he often stayed up even later to send a few more e-mails or complete a final piece of work before nodding off on the couch. He'd move into his bedroom sometime during the night if he woke up. If not, he'd find himself in the morning stiff from sleeping on the floor or couch. When we asked him what his favorite outside-of-work activity was, he replied without hesitation, "Sleep."

When Glenn completed our Well-Being At-a-Glance Self-Assessment, his results pointed to an urgent need to renew his energy and take better care of himself physically. Initially, he questioned the results, confident that his current habits had served him well throughout most of his career. His stamina enabled him to muscle through most days. No health crisis appeared to be on the horizon. He admitted that he'd like to lose some weight but didn't perceive his weight as a risk to his overall well-being.

Glenn didn't buy that poor health compromised his leadership. In fact, he suggested that his work habits were the only way he could lead his team, fulfill his own tactical work commitments, and attend the meetings in which he was expected to participate. It wasn't until his staff voiced their concerns that his choices were negatively affecting them that Glenn paused to a take a deeper look at the connection between his health habits and his leadership.

He'd lobbied two members to take on greater responsibilities and consider a promotion to management, and both declined. When pressed, they confessed that Glenn's work schedule had convinced them that leadership was not for them. They wanted to maintain some balance in their lives. With Glenn's model of leadership, they didn't see that balance as even possible. Glenn finally realized at a visceral level that his habits were standing in the way of growing his team's leadership capacity. His long hours and unbalanced lifestyle telegraphed a loud message to his team members: *to lead in this office, you need to exhaust yourself and give up on a life outside of work.* The wake-up call he'd ignored for so long had finally rung loud enough for him to hear it.

With new and sincere resolve, Glenn began to uncover and examine the habits that undermined his body's well-being. Together, we looked at his exercise, eating, and sleep habits. Eating processed food mindlessly in front of the television late at night, working out only once or twice a week for a short time, and consistently getting short-changed on sleep were just a few of the habits that eroded his energy and health.

Glenn questioned whether he'd have the discipline to sustain any meaningful changes. He surprised himself. He discovered that in the process of naming those beliefs and behaviors that he needed to let go of or shift, he created the space for new habits to take hold and grow. He committed to turning off his computer by 9:00 P.M. each evening and falling asleep in his bed rather than on his living room couch. He arranged to meet a friend at the gym several evenings a week after work so that he'd feel more accountable for showing up consistently. As he began to feel more rested and better nourished, he noticed he could think more creatively about how he could better delegate to his team, which enabled him to take less work home at night. His team members noticed the changes as well. They stepped up and took on more responsibilities, which freed Glenn to focus on bigger strategic priorities.

Your Turn

1. What are the red flags that signal you may be in a pattern of sacrificing your well-being?
   - Is it going for the third cup of coffee or unhealthy food in the late afternoon to give yourself an energy boost?
   - Responding impatiently to family members?
   - Overreacting to situations that are small in scope?
   - Sacrificing exercise to spend one more hour responding to e-mails?
   - Cutting short time spent with loved ones to spend more time at the office?

2. Write down your red-flag habits and post them somewhere easy to see. Check in with yourself on a daily basis—which red flags are manifesting for you on a consistent basis?

3. Glenn believed that sacrificing his own wellness was the price he needed to pay for achieving success in his role. To what extent do you hold this same belief? How might it be getting in your way?

When leaders complete our Well-Being At-a-Glance worksheet, they frequently find that their physical wellness needs their immediate attention. They acknowledge that they've been tolerating their own unhealthy eating habits for far too long. They've been missing out on the benefits of consistent exercise. They deprive themselves of necessary sleep and rejuvenation. Most of us know intuitively that healthy bodies mean healthier lives—and science backs up common sense.

In a Nutshell: What We Know about Healthy Bodies

Exercise: An Addiction with Benefits

In his book *Spark,* clinical associate professor of psychiatry at Harvard Medical School John J. Ratey, MD, points to scientific evidence of the benefits of physical exercise on brain health, ability to learn, and emotional well-being.[1] Physical exercise, it turns out, doesn't just help you lose weight, build muscle, or increase your stamina; a fitter body leads to a fitter brain.

Exercise, both aerobic and strength building, acts like Miracle Gro for the brain, triggering the release of proteins such as BDNF (brain-derived neurotropic factor), which functions like fertilizer for your neurons. This neurotransmitter, along with others, sparks the development of new nerve cells in the hippocampus area of your brain, increasing your potential to learn and function more efficiently.

Ratey also explains that the parts of the brain that coordinate motor movements, like returning a tennis serve, are the same parts of the brain that help you learn a new language. When you strengthen those neurons through physical exercise, you increase your brain's capacity to learn and retain new information because the two different activities employ the same neural circuitry.

How important is it for you as a leader to learn and retain new information? To function at a high level of alertness and energy? Ratey highlights studies that suggest that if you're in good shape, you may be able to learn and function more efficiently.

How critical is it for you to project a positive mood and emotions to those you lead? Exercise, Ratey indicates, has been proven to elevate the neurotransmitters in the brain, like dopamine, that facilitate positive emotions and a more resourceful and optimistic mood. Studies show that the higher your fitness level, the less likely you are to feel anxiety and stress.

Take a moment now to assess your own exercise routine. How often are you making time for physical exercise? Do you include aerobic and strength-building activities? Are you having fun and challenging yourself while you exercise? Finding a form of exercise that you enjoy will make it easier to sustain your commitment over time.

Sleep: The Costs of Deprivation

Perhaps you're easily persuaded about the value that exercise has on your well-being, but how convinced are you of the importance of sleep in your ability to function successfully as a leader?

If recent studies are any indication, Americans are increasingly sleep deprived, and our sleep habits are exacting a dangerous toll. Fatal airplane pilot errors and catastrophic car accidents have been directly tied to sleep deprivation.[2] Increasing rates of insomnia and disturbed sleep have led to the explosive growth of the sleep-aid industry. As a population, we're overtired and overwired. We're turning to energy drinks and sleep medications to combat our fatigue.

How much sleep do you get most nights? What's the quality of your sleep? When you wake up in the morning, do you feel rested? If not, what's the impact on your mood and energy during the day? How does your sleep deprivation influence your reactions and the actions you take?

According to a recent Centers for Disease Control and Prevention report, nearly one-third of working adults in the United States get less than six hours of sleep a night. David Randall reports in a 2012 *Wall Street Journal* article that this number of sleep-deprived adults marks a 25 percent increase since 1990.

Does it really matter if you sacrifice sleep to achieve just a bit more during the day? Because we live in a culture that largely believes that sleep is something we can put off, we're all susceptible to the assumption that sacrificing pillow time is something we can get away with.

But science suggests that sleeplessness and sleep deprivation impair the immune system, sabotage creativity, and contribute to increased rates of heart disease, obesity and stroke, and even certain cancers. Recent studies reveal that sleep loss increases cravings for processed, sugary foods over fruit and vegetables. The less you sleep, the less you have energy to exercise, sending you into a cycle of trying to compensate in unhealthy, unproductive ways for your fatigue. Sleep deprivation negatively impacts mood, alertness, and performance.

Do any of these alarming facts inspire you to adjust your own sleep habits?

If so, there are simple steps you can take to shift the dial and ensure you're getting more of the recommended seven to nine hours of restful sleep that the National Sleep Foundation indicates that you need to lead with energy, stamina, and focus:

- Pay attention to how much sleep you are typically getting. If it's routinely less than six hours, you need to make a change.
- Avoid caffeine in the late afternoon or evening.
- Turn off screens—TV, computer, and phone—at least an hour before bedtime. They simulate the experience of daylight for your body, and the stimulation makes it harder for your body and brain to drift off to sleep.
- Exercise in the morning so you can fall asleep more easily at night.

Restful sleep will equip you to lead with more stamina and energy. You'll accomplish more. Positive moods are within easier reach, too, when your body is well rested.

Mindful Eating: Leadership and Nourishment

Most of the leaders with whom we work focus all their energy and attention on getting important work done—and that means they skip meals, eat on the fly, and pay little attention to what they're eating and whether it's nourishing them.

Do you finish your meals long before your family, friends, or colleagues finish theirs? Do you find yourself grabbing a bag of chips and a diet soda to wash them down in between meetings instead of eating a healthy lunch? Are you missing meals altogether? Has eating become just one more task to accomplish in the day rather than an activity that nourishes and replenishes you?

What if eating and nourishing yourself took on greater importance in your routine? If you tasted the food you were eating and slowed down the pace of your eating, would you improve your overall well-being?

Try introducing these two easy-to-implement practices for encouraging mindfulness in your eating habits and improving your overall health:

Ask yourself, "Am I hungry?" Many people are lucky enough to have access to more than enough food to nourish their bodies—and eat out of boredom, anxiety, or other emotions rather than real hunger. The habit of overeating or eating mindlessly can be broken when you ask yourself this simple question and check in with your body for the answer.

Pay attention. For the next week, when you eat, avoid reading, watching TV, or working on your computer. Focus on the experience of eating. Savor the food you're tasting. Chew more slowly and pause between bites. As you bring more attention to what and how you're eating, you'll enjoy the experience of eating more. You'll be more aware of when your stomach is satisfied and you're no longer hungry. After one week, notice what's different, if anything, about your eating habits and their impact on your energy and well-being.

Now is the time to be ruthlessly honest with yourself and recognize what habits you need to address and change. How do your habits align with the guidelines for exercise, sleep, and mindful eating that we've shared here?

When you're a leader, others scrutinize your habits closely. If you consistently short-change your welfare, you're essentially reinforcing a belief in your organization that generating positive results requires leaders to sacrifice their health and wellness. If in your heart you believe otherwise, your next step is to commit to new practices and actions that align your intentions with your actual behavior.

Phase 3: Develop Practices That Nurture and Support Your Well-Being

As Richard Strozzi-Heckler writes in *The Leadership Dojo,* how we show up in our leadership and our lives is a reflection of our habits.[3] We are the habits we practice. If we practice sacrificing our well-being, we will be depleted. If we practice caring for ourselves, we will become healthier in mind, body, heart, and spirit. We regain our vitality when we practice habits that support our wellness.

What practices are part of your well-being routine? If we interviewed one of your trusted family members, friends, or colleagues about your wellness, what might they say? You may be unaware of the habits you're practicing that erode your well-being, but they're often obvious to those who live and work alongside you.

Remember Aesop's fable about the ant and grasshopper? The ant methodically prepares food stores for the long winter months, while the grasshopper idles away his time during the summer and faces the harsh winter with no reserves. Aesop reminds us that what we practice now has implications for what we will enjoy in the future.

Introducing and sustaining practices that nurture and support your well-being is vital to deepening your satisfaction in your leadership and life. Follow our client Rita's story and learn how the practices she intentionally launched increased her energy both at home and at work.

The Power of the Positive: Rita's Story

A social worker by training, Rita had assumed the leadership mantle when the former executive director of her organization retired. As she took on more and more responsibilities that were new and unfamiliar to her, she spent more and more of her time at her office. Even during her family time after work, she found her mind wandering. She fretted constantly about projects she'd left undone. Her sleep was fitful. In the mornings, she woke without feeling rested. Profound exhaustion became her norm.

When we began our work together, Rita articulated several clear and compelling agendas for leadership coaching. She wanted to regain balance in her life, cultivate more calm in her role, and build her confidence in her capacity to lead her organization successfully. She already trusted her relationship-building skills and felt proud of the team she'd developed. She didn't question her ability to lead her team effectively but rather her ability to manage her anxiety and self-doubt. Her goals for coaching largely centered on tending to her well-being and introducing sustainable practices that would support her mental and emotional health and inspire her spirit.

After an initial well-being self-assessment, Rita acknowledged that her healthy exercise and eating habits had helped her only up to a certain point. Peace of mind and a renewed commitment to lead were what she longed for most.

In our first few conversations, Rita identified self-management and self-regulation as the skills areas she most wanted to improve. If she could find healthier ways to recognize and work with her emotions and self-doubt, she was convinced she would lead with more confidence and ease.

Rita introduced and sustained certain key practices designed to help her recognize and manage negative emotions and calm her nervous system. Before she arrived at her office, she began her day in quiet reflection. She gave herself a few minutes to use a Centering practice (see page 214 in the appendix) to relax her body, ground herself, and formulate her intention for the day. She spent another five minutes with her eyes closed, focusing on her breath. She learned that her mind wandered often, as our minds are designed to do. Worries about the day ahead and feelings of inadequacy often surfaced during these few minutes of mindfulness meditation. We coached her simply to notice her wandering mind and her emotions nonjudgmentally. We suggested she could treat her attention like a muscle she wanted to exercise and bring it back to her breath every time she became aware of its wandering.

In our conversations about her emotional well-being, we explained to Rita that humans are not designed to access positive emotions easily or in a sustainable way.

The good news we shared with Rita is that because of the brain's capacity to build new neural pathways constantly, we have the ability to reshape the brain's tendencies through intentional practice. As neuropsychiatrist Dr. Dan Siegel points out, through specific practices, we can use our awareness and attention to establish new neural pathways in the brain and new habits of thinking in the mind.[4]

Rita was eager and open to adopt new practices that would enrich her mental, emotional, and spiritual well-being. She began to document her "wins" at the end of each day, however small they might appear. She launched a new habit of recognizing and sustaining her positive emotions over a longer period of time by paying more attention to her positive experiences when they occurred and tuning in to how they affected her physically. And she began a yoga practice that she consistently followed at least three times a week—although she'd always been devoted to a rigorous exercise regimen, she discovered that yoga better met her desire to quiet her worrying mind.

Because Rita followed her new practices with discipline and devotion, she started to notice herself experiencing more ease and less anxiety about her work. Her self-confidence increased and she found more satisfaction in her successes. She took on a new project at work, a major fund-raising initiative, and found herself excited about the effort and free from the worry that would have nagged at her previously. She learned that she could proactively influence her well-being through vigilant practice and that she and her organization benefited dramatically from her focused efforts.

Your Turn

1. Find a quiet place where you can practice the seated mindfulness meditation practice we call STILL for at least three to five uninterrupted minutes. You might set a timer for yourself so you don't have to monitor the time.

   S = **Sit** quietly
   Sit upright on a cushion or chair with your eyes closed. Lengthen your spine and hold your chin slightly up and parallel to the floor so that your body is awake and alert.

   T = Release **tension**
   Bring your attention to your body and notice where your muscles might be contracted. Gently release any tension. The area around the eyes, the brow, the jaw, and the shoulders are typically places in the body where we hold tension.

   I = **Inhale**
   As you take your next breath, make sure you extend your exhale so that all of the air is released from your lungs and your diaphragm deflates. On your next inhale, you'll be able to breathe in more deeply and from your belly.

   L = **Let go**
   Extend your next exhale, and as you do so, imagine that any tension or worry in your body and mind is dissolving.

L = **Lead your attention** back to your breath
Focus your attention on your breath. When your attention wanders away, simply lead it back to your breath without judgment. Do this as many times as necessary until your three to five minutes are complete.

2. Ask yourself the following questions:
    - What's the quality of my energy right now?
    - What's the quality of my presence right now?
    - How would it benefit me to be in this practice more often?

In a Nutshell: What We Know about Building Wellness in Our Mind and Spirit

The data is in and it's conclusive. Spending time in quiet contemplation, or mindfulness meditation, reduces emotional reactivity, improves resilience, and builds new neural pathways that strengthen the ability to focus. Mindfulness meditation has now become more widely accepted and practiced in Western culture, including in corporations, schools, and organizations.

Take, for example, the corporation Google. Since 2007, Google has offered the Search Inside Yourself (SIY) program to its leaders and employees. Sponsored by Chade-Meng Tan, one of Google's original engineers, and developed with the help of a Zen master, a Stanford University scientist, a CEO, and Daniel Goleman, an expert in emotional intelligence, SIY is a seven-week course that incorporates mindfulness meditation training into its curriculum. More than one thousand Google employees have attended the program so far, and there's a waiting list for every course offering.[5]

How comfortable are you with the practice of sitting quietly and focusing your attention? How easy is it for you to sit in stillness, follow your breath, and refocus your attention when it wanders?

Like some of the leaders we coach, you may find this practice uncomfortable. You may resist the idea of taking even a few minutes to focus your awareness away from your to-do list. Maybe you're thinking that you simply don't have the ten or fifteen minutes needed to sit in meditative silence.

What if you knew that mindfulness meditation has been proven to reshape your brain and that people who routinely practice meditation access more positive emotions, worry less, recover more quickly from setbacks, and experience more satisfaction in life generally? If your leadership success and effectiveness include being a calm presence for your team and responding thoughtfully to circumstances rather than reacting to them, then mindfulness meditation is a practice that can serve you well.

THE WELL-BEING CONVERSATION: KEY TAKEAWAYS

To be a successful leader requires an energetic body, an open heart, a calm mind, and an enlivened spirit. When you engage your body, mind, heart, and spirit in regular renewal, you become more adept at calling forth others' best efforts as well as your own. Ignoring your well-being comes at a price. You cannot rally others or perform at your best without energy, clarity, optimism, and meaning.

The Well-Being Conversation is written for you and other talented and dedicated leaders who put their wellness on the line day in and day out. In this chapter, you asked yourself the question "How am I?" and uncovered the areas of your well-being that are starved for attention. You named those habits and tendencies that undermine your health and vigor, and you landed on new habits that will revitalize you. Whether it's regular exercise, healthier eating choices, mindfulness meditation, or other practices that encourage your joy and contentment, you're now better positioned to model well-being for your team and organization.

The Well-Being Conversation: What's Next?

Coaching Assignments for Leveraging Your Learning

Is the Well-Being Conversation particularly critical for you? The following list of Actions, Practices, and Resources is a tool kit for engaging more deeply in this important Missing Conversation.

Action Steps

- Consider inviting someone close to you, perhaps a spouse or partner or a trusted friend, to reflect on his view of your well-being and complete the Well-Being At-a-Glance Self-Assessment on your behalf.
    - What does this person's assessment of your well-being reveal to you?
    - Are there discrepancies between this person's perception of your well-being and your own? If so, how do you explain them?
- Complete the Wheel of Well-Being on page 217 in the appendix as another way to identify and target those areas of your well-being you want to focus on.
- Find an accountability partner for your exercise routine—someone who commits to exercise with you on a consistent basis.

Ongoing Practices

- Start your day off by asking yourself the simple yet powerful question "How am I?" As you sit with this question for a few minutes, check in with your body, mind, heart, and spirit.
- At either the end of your workday or the beginning of the following workday, reflect on the "wins" you achieved that day and document them for yourself. The size or significance of your win doesn't matter. This practice centers on acknowledging any success you can feel proud of.
- Introduce the STILL mindfulness meditation practice into your everyday routine. Start with a five-minute practice and gradually lengthen your STILL practice so that you cultivate the capacity to focus your attention and rest in awareness for increasing lengths of time. Search online for free guided meditations that work for you.

Suggested Resources

Buddha's Brain: The Practical Neuroscience of Happiness, Love, and Wisdom by Rick Hanson, PhD, with Richard Mendius, MD: New Harbinger, 2009.

The Emotional Life of Your Brain: How Its Unique Patterns Affect the Way You Think, Feel, and Live—and, How You Can Change Them by Richard Davidson, PhD, and Sharon Begley: Hudson Street Press, 2012.

Thrive: The Third Metric to Redefining Success and Creating a Life of Well-Being, Wisdom, and Wonder by Arianna Huffington: Christabella, 2014.

The Way We're Working Isn't Working: The Four Forgotten Needs That Energize Great Performance by Tony Schwartz: Free Press, 2010.

CHAPTER 6

Where Do I Go from Here? The Career Crossroads Conversation

Deep within us lies an awareness of what shape our life is to take.

—**Wayne Dyer**

The Capacity and Well-Being Conversations ask you to check in with yourself on a weekly or even daily basis. When you regularly ask yourself, "How much is enough?" and adjust your capacity accordingly, or when you consistently pay attention to the state of your well-being, you're better able to make critical course corrections that support your leadership and your life.

The Career Crossroads Conversation is as crucial, but its timing works differently. It's seasonal in nature and tied to the particular circumstances or place in your career in which you find yourself. The core question you'll explore in this chapter is "Where do I go from here?" If you are feeling increasingly restless in your work or leadership, or are longing for something more, it could be the single most important conversation you engage in.

When you are standing at a career crossroads, you typically find yourself asking questions for which you have no easy or clear answers. You might be wondering whether you want to stay with your organization or venture elsewhere, take on a brand-new role that's been offered to you, or head in a different direction altogether. Perhaps you're asking yourself even more fundamental questions like "What do I really want?" "Am I really happy?" or "Do I really want to lead?"

Because you are reading this chapter, chances are that you have some unanswered questions about your path. For most people, this state of uncertainty is not particularly comfortable.

Imagine for a moment that you are driving in an unfamiliar city toward a busy four-way intersection on a major highway. As you approach the intersection, you notice signs indicating a detour ahead. Your navigation system tells you to go straight, and the detour tells you to turn. Suddenly you aren't sure which way you should go or what lane you should be in. The light turns green, but you are stalled, trying to figure out whether you should follow the detour or continue straight ahead. Impatiently, the cars behind you begin to honk, and you feel forced to make a decision, unsure if it's the right one.

How do you feel in this situation? Unnerved? Frustrated? Anxious? Perhaps you are worried that your decision, if made hastily, will take you down a dead-end road. This literal crossroads experience in many ways mirrors the feelings and challenges of a career crossroads. In both cases, you are faced with decisions or choices that you may feel unprepared or ill equipped to make.

You can find yourself at a career crossroads for myriad reasons:

- You feel stuck or stagnant in your current role
- Your organization is going in a direction with which you no longer agree
- You've undergone significant changes on the home front that are causing you to reevaluate your work
- You have urges or longings to do something different that you can no longer quiet or ignore

What brings you to *your* crossroads?

During your lifetime, you will likely face several turning points or crossroads in your career—times when you are feeling restless, unsure of the path you are on, and not clear about what's next for you. The Crossroads Conversation gives you the tools to navigate these turning points well and ensures that your next step is the right one for you.

Your direct reports will have to navigate their own set of crossroads. Part of your job as a leader is to help your employees face and move through these crossroads as quickly and as thoughtfully as possible, so that the right people are in the right jobs and those who aren't a good fit can find opportunities elsewhere. The exercises and resources included in this chapter are designed to help you determine your next step, but they're also tools you can share with those you coach and mentor.

What happens if you don't take the time to evaluate thoughtfully the path you're on, or to help those who work for you do the same? In our experience, people end up making one of two mistakes: they either jump ship prematurely, without truly knowing what they want, and land someplace else that isn't any better for them—or they hunker down and stay put, hoping something around them will change. When nothing does, they can end up feeling trapped and resentful. Thinking they have no choice but to muster on, they continue to show up for work, but without their previous level of engagement or commitment.

Missing the Crossroads Conversation means ending up on the sidelines of your work or your life. You're not really in the game—and not really out of it, either.

Although you may feel alone as you wrestle with your own crossroads dilemma, take some comfort in knowing that many others have faced similar turning points and have come out on the other side with their vision clearer and their sense of hope for the future restored. The good news is that the answers you seek are within your grasp. To access this wisdom that lies deep within *you,* read on. We'll walk you through the three phases of the Career Crossroads Conversation, which will enable you to develop greater clarity around your next step, along with the courage and confidence to take it.

PHASE 1: STEP BACK AND TAKE STOCK

Whatever your reason for being at a crossroads, we invite you to consider this time and place as a gift. Instead of rushing headlong into your next move, or allowing the inertia of your present situation to carry you along, we encourage you to step back and take stock. This is your chance to consider thoughtfully which path forward is truly best for you.

We've found that many of our clients want to identify and explore options first, before they have assessed where they are and what they really want. This is what we call an "outside-in" approach to navigating a career crossroads: you look "out there" in your organization or in the marketplace to see what jobs or roles are available and then try to match yourself to those opportunities. This approach can lead you to choose roles or organizations that aren't a good fit.

We advocate an "inside-out" approach instead.[1] This means looking within yourself first to get clarity about what you do best, what you care about most, and when and where you naturally thrive. Once you know yourself better and are clear about what constitutes your ideal work, you can make wiser choices about your future.

The following seven elements have a significant impact on your career success and satisfaction. Think of them as pieces of a puzzle. When you put them together, you create a clear picture of your best work. Which of these career elements might be important for you to revisit and clarify at this particular crossroads?

1. *Talents and abilities*. Your innate gifts that emerged very early in your life. They can be qualities you possess, like a tendency toward optimism, or natural abilities, such as a knack for problem solving. Assessments like Gallup's Strengths Finder 2.0 and the Highlands Ability Battery (both listed in the coaching tool kit at the back of this chapter) can be helpful tools for naming and identifying your natural talents.
2. *Strengths*. The specific activities you excel at *and* that energize you.[2] It's important to distinguish strengths from *skills*. Skills are things

you have learned to do well through training or experience but that you may or may not enjoy. The Gallup organization's research on strengths has shown that employees who are able to do what they do best every day are "six times as likely to be engaged in their jobs and more than three times as likely to report having an excellent quality of life in general."[3]

3. *Values.* The principles for which you stand and the things that make work and life meaningful. For example, do you value excellence? Creativity? Innovation? A crossroads crisis can emerge when you realize that your values are no longer in sync with your organization's or if the actual work you do no longer aligns with what you value most. If you would like some additional help clarifying this essential element, please see the values exercise on page 21 in chapter 1.
4. *Interests and passions.* The things about which you are naturally curious and that you find intrinsically interesting. Some of your interests may find an outlet in a hobby, while others may be expressed at work. Interests and passions bring energy and vitality to your career and enrich your life. To what extent does your work (and your personal life) reflect what you are most interested in and passionate about?
5. *Temperament.* Your basic personality preferences, style, and tendencies. For example, do you get energy from being around a lot of people or from quiet solitude? Are you naturally comfortable with conflict and chaos or drained by it? A role or environment that requires you to go against your natural temperament on a consistent basis often leads to burnout.
6. *Purpose.* Your core mission or reason for being. Why are you here and what contribution do you most want to make? Is the work you do a good vehicle for you to express this purpose? If not, how much does this matter to you?
7. *Personal requirements.* This may include things like salary needs, strong preferences for where you live and work, or the length of your commute.

The more your work is aligned with these seven elements, the more satisfied you tend to be and, ultimately, the more effective you are. However, human beings evolve over time, and so does our work. Sometimes, without our awareness or explicit consent, the gap between who we are and what we do every day widens, leaving us increasingly restless, yet unclear as to why.

This certainly was the case for Jane, a senior project manager. As you read her story, notice how exploring the preceding elements helped her regain a clearer and more optimistic view of herself and her future options.

Soul Searching: Jane's Story

Jane was facing a crossroads that had been in the making for some time. For the last twelve years, she had worked as a senior project manager at a large aerospace company, but she no longer found the work fulfilling. In fact, for the past three years, she had found herself increasingly disengaged and emotionally checked out. Jane felt trapped by her good salary and the lack of clarity she had around other options. She also felt increasingly resentful of her situation and burdened by the financial obligations that had become her main reason for going to work every day. Deciding that she no longer wanted to work that way, Jane hired us to help her figure out what she really wanted and what she might do next.

The answers to those questions would take some significant soul searching on her part. In our first coaching session, Jane admitted, "I'm not sure who I am anymore and I don't know how to find out." Jane had spent the last several years behaving like a chameleon at work: molding herself to meet her boss's and her organization's expectations, with little regard for what she wanted or needed. Her biggest obstacle to figuring out what she should do next was that she had lost touch with herself.

To remedy this, we asked Jane to engage in the Career Crossroads Conversation. She began by completing a number of self-exploration assignments over the course of a few months. One of the first things we asked her to do was to collect various pictures, images, and phrases that captured her imagination and interest and to store them in a file. Jane was a visual learner and a photographer in her spare time. Although her logical, analytical mind didn't know who she was or what she wanted, her creative, artistic self did. After several weeks of collecting images, Jane turned her clippings into a collage. Though the collage didn't tell her exactly what her next step should be, it was an inspiring visual reminder of her true interests and passions.

Another key assignment Jane undertook involved tracking her flow states—those times when she was absorbed and engaged in her work—as well as those times she felt drained by it. Jane made notes about what she was doing in those moments and who was involved. By observing and tracking her engagement highs and lows during the week, Jane was able to pinpoint more specifically what she liked and disliked about her work and what kinds of activities called forth her best efforts.

Jane discovered that she lost energy when she had to deal with office politics, solve interpersonal conflicts, or work remotely in isolation (a by-product of the increasing number of virtual teams at her workplace). In contrast, she discovered she was energized when she had clear, challenging goals to execute, was in charge of leading a meaningful project or cause, had a variety of tasks to work on, and had the freedom to make her own decisions regarding her teams. Jane began to see more clearly that she needed variety, visibility, and feedback to be at her best and that these three things were very much lacking in her current work.

As Jane grew in her self-knowledge and understanding, she became more confident and assertive. She shared with her boss her new understanding of her job likes and dislikes and where she felt she could contribute most to the company. Rather than simply accepting whatever assignments came her way, she asked her boss if she could take the lead on a new cross-functional project that would engage her strengths and provide greater face-to-face contact with her team. She also learned some strategies for dealing more effectively with office politics so that they wouldn't drain her as much.

Jane also began to make a series of small but important changes in her personal life. She enrolled in a photography class, began reaching out to old friends to socialize more, and resigned from a volunteer board position she held that had been draining her. Although these moves didn't change her work situation, they did improve her overall outlook and gave her a greater sense of being in control of her life.

Jane explored a number of alternative career options and had a few conversations with people in these other fields to learn more about them. Ultimately, she decided they weren't the right fit for her. Jane wasn't ready for a big career change. Instead, she wanted to try her hand at some new projects and see if she could reshape her current role enough so that it more fully aligned with what she did best and cared about most.

When we last saw her, Jane reported that she had become much less of a chameleon at work. She was engaged in a new, highly visible long-term assignment that was giving her some much-needed variety, and she was not feeling as stuck. "I now know that I have options, that there isn't only one answer or way forward, and that I have more influence over my work than I previously realized," she told us. Jane chose to continue with her organization but vowed to revisit her situation and take stock again in another year. At that time she might decide to leave, but for now she was feeling more content, productive, and hopeful than she had in years.

Your Turn

The central question of the Career Crossroads Conversation is "Where do I go from here?" Before you answer that question, it's helpful to know where "here" is. Use the following reflections to assess your current situation.

1. Career crossroads are often characterized by feeling stuck, stagnant, or restless. To what extent is this true for you? Take a few moments to complete the Career Satisfaction Self-Assessment on page 128 and discuss your results with a trusted mentor or confidant. What do your results reveal to you about the extent and source of your restlessness? What do they say about what's working and not working in this season of your career?

2. Jane's story shows that sometimes the answer to a crossroads dilem-

ma is not to change jobs or careers but rather to change the way you approach your work and life. What small changes might you make to reduce your frustrations or improve your level of satisfaction at work or at home? Take the time to identify *at least one*.

3. Jane engaged in a series of conversations with her immediate manager to shift her assignments so that they played more to her strengths and interests. When was the last time you talked to your manager about your own career success and satisfaction? Are there specific requests you might make to steer your work in a direction that's more satisfying for you?

CAREER SATISFACTION SELF-ASSESSMENT

To help you get a better sense of your current level of career/job satisfaction, take a minute to rate yourself on a scale of 1 to 5 for each of the following statements. Then total your score below.

1 = Not true at all *2 = Rarely true* *3 = Sometimes true*
4 = Mostly true *5 = Always true*

____ I look forward to going to work most mornings.
____ I enjoy the work I do.
____ I enjoy the people with whom I work.
____ I am learning, growing, and being challenged on the job.
____ I respect my boss and have a good working relationship with him or her.
____ My core values mesh well with my organization's core values.
____ I am supportive of the direction my organization is going in and the strategy we are using to get there.
____ I feel hopeful about my future and the career opportunities that lie ahead of me.
____ I am well regarded and my expertise is sought after in my organization.
____ I am making the kind of contribution I want and believe I am capable of making.

YOUR TOTAL SCORE: ________

If your score is 25 or lower, you may be at a crossroads in your career, regardless of whether you have faced it yet. Even a score of 30–35 may indicate that you are not as engaged, productive, or satisfied in your work as you want to be and could benefit from thoughtfully considering the path you're on. Although you may still be showing up for work every day, if your score is low, chances are good that you may have already checked out emotionally.

Facing and Owning Your Career Crossroads Journey

As renowned management expert and author Peter Senge says, "leadership exists when people are no longer victims of circumstances but participate in creating new circumstances."[4] A vital turning point in Jane's journey came when she decided to face her crossroads situation head-on and proactively do something about it. Rather than continuing to ignore her feelings of frustration and discontent, or to blame others for her circumstances, she chose to take full responsibility for the quality and trajectory of her career. In essence, she decided to be the force for change in her own life.

Sometimes people forfeit this responsibility, inadvertently allowing (or even expecting) their company, their boss, or external events to define them or to determine their next steps. One of our clients admitted to us, "Sometimes I wish someone else was in charge of my life and would tell me what to do next with my career, even though I know that I am the only one who can."

How do you know if you've decided to be the force for change in your life? A good indication is that you are able let go of any resentment, blame, or resignation you may have about the crossroads that you currently face. You feel you have a choice about where you're headed next. Before reading any further in this chapter, pause for a moment and consider the extent to which this describes you. If it does not, what might you do to change this?

Phase 2: Explore Options That Are a Good Fit for You

As you stand at your crossroads, what options do you see in front of you? Now that you've begun to take stock of where you are and what you really want, identifying options that are a good fit should be a little easier. Which of these choices might you be considering at this time?

- *Career tune-up*. Like Jane, you might decide to continue on your current path but choose to do so with a different mind-set or a slight tweaking of your role so that the path you're traveling is easier to navigate, more enjoyable, and more fulfilling.

- *Career upgrade.* Is a promotion to the next level of leadership on your horizon? If so, how does this move align with what you do best and care about most?
- *Slight turn in direction.* Another option is to do similar work at a different organization. Perhaps it's time to move on and stretch your wings someplace else or look for a new role to play in your current organization. Are either of these slight turns worth considering for you?
- *Hard left or right turn.* Perhaps more significant changes are called for. Does it make sense for you to change both *what* you are doing and *where* you are doing it? This could mean taking on a new role at a different organization or even in a different industry. While you change the nature and location of your work, you continue to utilize your existing skills and experience.
- *Go off-road.* This last choice requires a willingness to take risks and a tolerance for uncertainty, which not everyone has the nerve or the financial portfolio to support. When you choose this option, you pursue a long-held dream, such as starting your own business, and you work to build the support structure and new skills you'll need to succeed. You'll learn more about this option a bit later when you read Pam's story in phase 3.

Whereas Jane opted for a career tune-up and chose to stay with her organization, your crossroads journey may lead you to other destinations. Such was the case for another of our clients, an attorney who was working toward becoming a partner at a law firm when she decided to take another path instead. As you read Meg's story, pay particular attention to how identifying her natural abilities and strengths helped her to navigate her crossroads journey.

Capitalizing on Strengths: Meg's Story

When Meg began working with us, she already knew that she wanted to be doing something different professionally. She was a well-paid lawyer in a successful law firm, but she was unhappy, stressed at work, and feeling increasingly out of sync with her firm. Her dissatisfaction was also affecting her home life. Meg often found herself distracted, tense, and unable to be fully present with her family.

We began our work together by exploring the times in her career when she had felt most productive and engaged. Meg recalled a time about four years earlier when she was more heavily involved in planning, strategizing, and interacting with other lawyers and defendants. During this time, she did "eight different things every day," was engaged in complex problem solving daily, and could see tangible results from the work she was doing. Although she was involved in some research, she spent most of her time engaging with clients or planning strategy.

In contrast, she spent the bulk of her current days researching and writing, two tasks in which she was talented but that drained her. In the last year, her firm had changed direction, taking on more cases that were largely research based. The culture had also shifted, and Meg felt that the firm was rewarding people for working more hours but not necessarily for achieving results. Making partner in the firm would require her to take on more of the cases that left her drained and depleted and to work longer hours—something she lacked the motivation or desire to do.

Meg wanted to explore her natural abilities, so we suggested she complete an online assessment called the Highlands Ability Battery. Her results revealed that Meg was a diagnostic problem solver who could spot problems and see their solutions before anyone else could and who enjoyed a fast-paced, challenging work environment.

The Highlands Ability Battery also revealed that Meg was an Extroverted *Generalist.* Generalists crave variety in their work, prefer learning about a breadth of subjects to focusing on one in depth, and enjoy working as part of a team. As a strong extrovert, Meg got her energy from being around people. Her inherent nature as a Generalist and an Extrovert was at odds with the significant amount of research and writing she was doing on a daily basis. She sat at her desk for too much of the day, doing solitary work about 40 percent of the time. Meg was burning out as a result.

After completing the Highlands Ability Battery and reflecting on the projects and assignments that had given her the most success and satisfaction, Meg was able to distill her strengths into a clear list that included managing and setting strategy for complex cases, interacting with clients and gaining their trust, speaking to groups, and mentoring younger employees.

Meg was not spending much of her time doing these things in her current role, and she didn't see any real possibility of change. She began to identify other options outside her firm. She considered joining an in-house legal department in a large corporation and explored a job opening at the U.S. Attorney's Office. Neither of these options materialized.

After several weeks of networking, talking to people, and doing informational interviews, Meg found a new position in a nonprofit organization. Her role there required her to wear many hats (good for the Generalist in her) and to interact daily with outside stakeholders and investors (good for the Extrovert in her). The work was challenging, fast paced, and stimulating. Meg's new job played to her strengths and natural abilities.

After a couple of weeks in her new job, Meg's engagement and satisfaction with her work turned around. Another benefit was that she felt substantially less stressed and therefore took less stress home to her family. Although she still worked long hours, she had more energy to give on the home front and felt less stretched thin as a result.

Your Turn

1. Meg's job evolved into one that required her to spend a lot of time doing two things she was talented doing but didn't enjoy. Are there skills that you have learned to do well but don't enjoy? If so, how big of a role do they play in your current work?

2. What are your top three strengths? How much of your day do you spend using them?

3. Meg's firm changed its direction and shifted its culture, and she no longer felt aligned. Is the current direction and culture of your organization one that you embrace? If not, how might this disconnect be impacting your productivity and engagement?

Before moving forward with phase 3 of this conversation, we encourage you to pause and take another look at the five options we shared at the beginning of phase 2. In light of the stories you have read thus far and the reflections you have undertaken, which option at this point resonates most with you? Don't worry if you can't yet narrow it down. Just notice which paths are speaking to you more strongly, and why. Next we'll explore some potential stumbling blocks that may keep you from choosing your next move.

Phase 3: Choose Your Way Forward

In their book *Working on Yourself Doesn't Work,* Ariel and Shya Kane make a distinction between a *decision* and a *choice.*[5] Decisions, according to these authors, are heavily shaped by experience, history, and habits. They are often made without a deep awareness of the influencing factors and are sometimes carried out without much thought as to the short-term or long-term consequences. For example, you might make a decision to attend a particular school because that's where your parents went. Perhaps you decided to pursue a particular career because it gave you the status and lifestyle important to you or to others. On a smaller scale, you might decide to eat lunch at your desk one day and then keep doing that until it becomes a habit that you no longer question or reassess.

A *choice,* conversely, involves a different level of awareness and freedom. Choices are moves you make after you have honestly faced the questions and potential conflicts that are inherent in them. Although decisions can be made on autopilot, choices must be reflected on, wrestled with, and ultimately made with your eyes and heart wide open. They can lead you down new paths you haven't traveled before—paths that your history, experience, or logic alone wouldn't allow for.

This distinction is important in the Career Crossroads Conversation, particularly in phase 3. Once you have taken stock of where you are and have explored options that are a potential good fit, it's time to consciously *choose* your path. This can be challenging for a number of reasons, and it's not unusual to stumble on obstacles that make choosing and moving forward difficult.

Our client Pam's Career Crossroads Conversation involved facing those obstacles head-on before she could move forward. Regardless of what path you're taking, dealing with the inevitable roadblocks you may encounter along the way is key.

Letting Go of Fear: Pam's Story

Pam was a VP at a Hollywood film company who initially came to us for leadership coaching when she assumed a new role in her company. We worked with her for a few months as she transitioned into her new responsibilities and then didn't hear from her until a year later, when she contacted us again. This time Pam didn't want leadership coaching but rather help with a big decision: whether to stay with her company or launch out on her own.

Pam had been with her company for fourteen years. Earlier in her career, she had been motivated by the creative projects she led and the people she managed. But lately she found herself feeling increasingly frustrated in her role and more motivated by the paycheck than by the work itself. As a single woman, she didn't have a family at home to attend to, but the demands of her job often left her little time and energy on the weekends to do what she loved most: painting.

Pam was quite talented and had been featured in a number of art shows. As her fulfillment at work continued to decline, Pam's longing to paint grew stronger. She began to consider leaving her job to paint full time, but the thought terrified her. In one of our coaching sessions, we asked, "If you believed in yourself as the leader of your own life, what would you do?" She immediately responded, "Quit my job," and then quickly backtracked. "Well, at least take a day off!" It was becoming increasingly clear that her heart wasn't in her job as a VP and that something else was calling her.

We helped Pam explore a number of options, like working part time, taking a sabbatical, or finding another, less demanding job somewhere else. But it was clear that striking out on her own and trying to make it as a full-time artist was what she truly longed to do. Pam needed to address a number of obstacles and fears before she felt ready to make such a bold move.

One of the fears that she had to face was the fear of failure. What if people didn't like her art? What if she couldn't sell her paintings? What if she couldn't make it as an artist? Paradoxically, she also feared success. Would she lose contact with some of her current friends and family members if she became successful? Articulating her fears helped to loosen their grip on her.

Pam also had financial concerns. Her considerable salary allowed her a nice lifestyle. She was accustomed to being seen as successful by others and worried about how that might change if she left her job and the status and security it provided. Pam didn't know exactly what her financial situation was, so we encouraged her to meet with her financial advisor to get a better picture of her finances. Imagine her—and our—surprise when her advisor told her she could support herself at her present level with no income for five years! It turned out that Pam's financial fears—like many of our fears—were more in her head than grounded in reality.

Once Pam worked through her fears and began to dismantle them one by one, she become more emboldened and confident about her choice to be an artist full time. She knew she had the financial wherewithal to make this move, and now she had a newfound resolve to go with it. She gave her notice and never looked back. Five years later, she is a successful artist whose contemporary paintings continue to be featured at large and small art venues in California. Most importantly, she found a calling that challenges and fulfills her and has carved out a path that allows her to enjoy not only a good lifestyle but a good life as well.

Your Turn

1. What are your fears as you consider choosing among the options in front of you? Is there someone with whom you can talk about these fears who can help you to sort through them and loosen their grip on you?

2. Every career crossroads presents you with an opportunity to reassess your success-to-satisfaction ratio. How successful are you in terms of how you currently define success? How satisfied or fulfilled are you? Is the balance you have between these two things a good one for you? If not, what might you need to do to alter it?

3. If you have made a choice about where to go next at this crossroads but haven't yet acted upon it, what's holding you back? If there is roadblock or obstacle you need to tackle, resolve today to figure out what you can do to move it out of the way.

Navigating the Career Crossroads Conversation with self-awareness and skill ensures that you will continue to steer your work in a direction that is aligned with who you really are rather than in a direction that is best or expedient for others. You will likely face several crossroads in your career, and so will the people who report to you. How well you make your choices at these critical junctures greatly impacts your success and satisfaction. For this reason, the Career Crossroads Conversation is an essential one for your leadership and life.

The Career Crossroads Conversation: Key Takeaways

The Career Crossroads Conversation urged you to discern what shape your work and life should take. We invited you to face your current situation honestly and squarely, taking stock of what is and isn't working, to gain clarity about what you really want. We also encouraged you to face your fears about your potential next steps and to identify the stumbling blocks that may be holding you back. As you reflected on the puzzle pieces that constitute your ideal work, you reconnected with what you do best and care about most. This inside-out approach to navigating your crossroads enabled you to identify options that are a potential good fit for you and positions you to choose your next step wisely and with greater clarity and confidence.

The Career Crossroads Conversation: What's Next?

Coaching Assignments for Leveraging Your Learning

Is the Career Crossroads Conversation particularly critical for you? The following list of Actions, Practices, and Resources is a tool kit for engaging more deeply in this important Missing Conversation.

Action Steps

- Take one or two of the strengths-based assessments listed subsequently to gain new insight into your natural abilities and gifts. Ask a trusted mentor, coach, or colleague to read your results and debrief them with you. Use the insight you gain from your results to inform what you do next.
- Engage in a conversation with your boss about your current role and the degree to which it leverages your strengths. Ask for his or her feedback on what you do best and where your strengths can best be applied in your current organization. Share with him or her what you think your strengths are, how you might leverage them more fully, and what ideas you have for steering your work in a direction that is more aligned with what you do best and where you can contribute most.
- Engage in the Magic Wand Exercise: imagine that you've been given a magic wand and, with it, are able to redesign your current or future role in any way you want, as long as the changes you make enable you to do more of what you do best and care about most. What changes would you make to *what* you are doing, *how* you do it, and *whom* you work with? Which of these changes might be possible for you to make now?
- Reflect on your direct reports. Are any of them facing a career crossroads of their own? Do any of them seem checked out, restless, or disengaged? Are some of them in roles that don't play to their strengths? Engage in a coaching conversation with them, sharing what you've learned in this chapter.

Ongoing Practices

- Twice a week, reflect on your levels of engagement, energy, and flow at work. Were they consistently high throughout the week, or did they vary? When your engagement was high, what were you working on, and with whom? What about when it was low? Record your observations in a journal. Over time, this kind of attention will help you identify the work that brings forth your best efforts. Use this insight to guide your career in the direction that is most satisfying for you.
- Plan quarterly career satisfaction check-ins with yourself. Each quarter, take a morning or afternoon and go somewhere where you can reflect without distraction. Ask yourself three simple questions: (1) How happy and engaged am I at work these days? (2) What's working well? (3) What's not working well, and what changes might I make to course correct?

Suggested Resources

Do What You Are: Discover the Perfect Career for You through the Secrets of Personality Type by Paul D. Tieger and Barbara Barron-Tieger: Little, Brown, 1992.

Don't Waste Your Talent: The 8 Critical Steps to Discovering What You Do Best by Bob McDonald, PhD, and Don E. Hutchenson: The Highlands Company, 2005.

The Highlands Ability Battery (for more info on this assessment and to see a sample report, visit http://www.highlandsco.com)

In Search of the Perfect Job: 8 Steps to the $250,000+ Executive Job That's Right for You by Clyde C. Lowstuter: McGraw-Hill, 2007.

Now What? 90 Days to a New Life Direction by Laura Berman Fortgang: Penguin Books, 2004.

StrengthsFinder 2.0, by Tom Rath: Gallup Press, 2007 (Instructions and code for taking the StrengthsFinder assessment are included in the book)

PART III

Conversations That Accelerate Your Success

I attribute my success to this—I never gave or took any excuse.

—FLORENCE NIGHTINGALE

Despite the differences in their titles and expertise, the leaders we coach all share a common aspiration: to feel and be successful. How they define and measure success may look different depending on their situation, but at the end of the day, they are each driven by the desire to lead successfully.

Like you, these leaders wake up every morning with a picture of the day ahead of them. They start planning when they step into the shower; they set goals over their first cup of coffee. They formulate a list of tasks to accomplish as they're getting dressed.

But by the time the workday officially begins, reality has already thrown a wrench into the works. Unanticipated challenges are brewing even before they step into their offices. Personnel issues and customer crises hijack their carefully laid plans. Under these circumstances, even the most outwardly confident leaders begin to question if and how they can pull off victory.

It's easy to slip into discouragement or confusion when the sands shift around you. How do you sustain your success or take it to the next level when you're faced with challenges, unexpected change, or unforeseen setbacks? The three conversations you're about to undertake will point the way by focusing your attention on developing these essential elements:

- A vision that inspires you and others toward action
- A clear set of key priorities that holds your energy and attention
- The caring connections with others that make teamwork and trust possible

Get ready for transformation. The Inspiration, Strategic Focus, and Relationship conversations are a catalyst for your leadership success.

CHAPTER 7

What's the Better Future I See? The Inspiration Conversation

The leader is committed to a reality that doesn't exist yet; everyone else is quite content in the world as it exists now.

—**Len Schlesinger,** former president of Babson College and former Harvard professor

Inspirare, or "to breathe into," is the Latin root for the word *inspiration.* Breath is a fundamental source of life; without it, you cannot survive. To inspire, then, is to breathe new life into someone or something.

When was the last time you felt inspired at work or in your personal life? Pause for a moment to recall a time when you were uplifted, energized, or enlivened—by something beautiful you saw in nature, a conversation you had with a colleague, or an activity in which you engaged with your team. How did you feel in that moment? What new sensations, emotions, and thoughts emerged? What new possibilities became more accessible or available to you?

When you're inspired, a sense of hopefulness colors your thoughts and informs your actions. You're able to run more quickly, move more nimbly, and face obstacles with greater resolve. The opposite is also true: when you're uninspired and trying to conquer a challenging task, it's often like running a race with half your lung capacity—every step feels like a chore. Winning the race (or even completing it) feels difficult, if not impossible. You might eventually get there, but if you do, you'll most likely arrive out of breath and long after others have crossed the finish line.

In this chapter, we turn our attention to the fundamental way that leaders inspire their organizations: by envisioning and creating a shared future that people care about. When your team members *share* the better future you envision, they understand where you are leading them, are clear about why the future matters, and know what role they will play in creating it. And when they genuinely *care* about this shared future, they bring their full commitment and discretionary energy to making it happen. Creating a shared future that you and others care about is the essence of leadership—and it's hard work. The main reason it's challenging is built into the very nature of organizations themselves. All systems, from large corporations to biological organisms, are designed to preserve and protect the status quo. Breaking through this inertia requires boldness, clarity, and determination—along with a healthy dose of optimism.

To what extent are you inspiring your team to create a better future—one that you both genuinely care about? And if you're not, what's getting in your way?

Perhaps, like some of the leaders we've coached, you don't consider yourself to be an inspiration and therefore doubt your ability to engage others in a vision of the future. Maybe your time in the trenches has disconnected you from what you care about most and you are struggling to inspire yourself, let alone to inspire or uplift others. Or maybe you can envision a better, more exciting future, but you struggle with getting your team to make it theirs as well.

The Inspiration Conversation challenges you to breathe new life into your leadership and organization and requires your ongoing engagement.

Managing a business, organization or team involves inevitable ups and downs—but an inspired leader is prepared to take the long-term view through short-term crises. In the pages that follow, you'll meet three leaders who, like you, just needed to find the right spark—and the right strategic plan to make their shared future a shared reality.

Phase 1: Reconnect with What Enlivens You

If you fly with any regularity, you've heard the safety instructions that are given before takeoff plenty of times; in fact, you could probably recite them yourself, down to the part about donning your own oxygen mask before seeing to your child's. This, of course, makes perfect sense. After all, how can you support and assist others if you're struggling to breathe yourself? Embedded in this message is an important reminder, one that is fundamental to leading and to this conversation in particular: you must breathe life into your own leadership before you can truly inspire others.

To experience this firsthand, slow down your breathing until you're almost holding your breath. Continue to restrict your airflow by taking shallow, infrequent breaths for several seconds as you read this paragraph. How does it feel? After just a few moments of this restricted breathing pattern, you will probably notice your mind starting to lose focus and your body losing energy. All of your effort and attention are diverted into trying to make do with less air; there isn't much left over for focused attention, let alone for creative endeavors or bold declarations about the future. When you don't have enough oxygen, it is almost impossible to envision a hopeful or optimistic future. You're too busy trying to survive.

This certainly was true for our client Tina. Tina was in charge of a key change initiative aimed at creating a new future for her organization, but she was struggling to find the energy and optimism she needed to lead it. As you read about what she did to reinspire herself and others, consider how reconnecting with your own core purpose at work might also enliven you.

Coming Up for Air: Tina's Story

As the senior leader of a large retirement and senior care facility spread out over three campuses and serving five thousand residents, Tina was very busy. In addition to her regular responsibilities, she was asked to spearhead a culture change initiative in her organization, something she supported because of the collaborative work environment the initiative proposed. However, with everything else on her plate, culture change was quickly becoming one more action item on an already packed schedule.

When we first sat down with Tina, we asked her about the purpose of her work. "I started out in this business because I wanted to make a difference in people's lives," Tina told us. "This is why I get out of bed every day. But lately I wonder if I really am making a difference, and whether we are as an organization." She went on to explain that she spent much of her time in her office crunching numbers, writing reports, and doing budgets, all of which she found draining. Although she was good at rallying her team to achieve daunting goals, Tina admitted that she hadn't been doing much of that lately. Instead, she felt like she was treading water and just trying to make it through the week.

We knew Tina needed a breath of fresh air. We challenged her to get out of her office at least once each day, even if it was just for a few minutes, and to walk through the halls of the various buildings on her campus. We also suggested that she look for an opportunity to reconnect with her team in some meaningful way and to talk to people about what she cared about most.

When we met with her the following week, we found that Tina had taken our suggestions to heart. She had gotten out of her office and could see just how stretched thin her team was. Sensing her team's stress and strain, she canceled a two-hour budget meeting and told her staff to take that time to get out of their offices and connect with a resident, colleague, or associate. Do something that "makes you happy deep down in your soul," she told them, asking them to return ready to give their all to the challenges ahead. Tina wanted her team to engage openly and creatively in the upcoming culture change meetings, and she knew they needed to breathe some new life into their own leadership before they could.

This simple gesture had a profound impact on her team. Several of her direct reports told her how much her decision to cancel the meeting had meant to them. Connecting with residents and sharing their experiences with one another reinvigorated the team and injected a much-needed sense of purpose, clarity, and meaning into their week. For the first time in quite a while, Tina felt like she had made a difference.

Reconnecting with the people and sense of purpose that fueled her continued to bear fruit later that week when a crisis erupted in her facility. A well-loved resident died, and one of his family members threatened to file a lawsuit against Tina's facility, claiming neglect. When we sat down with her for her next coaching session after a particularly difficult and challenging week, we were surprised to find her more upbeat and energized than usual. It turned out that the crisis had required Tina to spend almost the entire week out of her office, interacting with residents, nurses, and other employees. She had been on-site each day solving challenging problems, giving her team direction, and offering much-needed support. At one point in the week, she found herself holding the hand of a terminally ill resident. As she sat at his bedside, she remembered the compassion and deep care that had been buried under mounting financial pressures and relentless paperwork. In that moment, she reawakened to her essential reason for working with and leading others.

Despite the challenges of her week, Tina felt more alive than she had in months. The administrative work had piled up in her absence from the office, and she still had to face all of it the next day. But she felt differently about it. She also felt more hopeful and committed to building a new culture and a new future for herself and her organization.

Before she entered into the Inspiration Conversation, Tina told us that she couldn't afford to leave her office and spend time on the floor with residents and staff. Afterward, she realized she couldn't afford *not* to. Now that she was reconnected to what she cared about most, Tina could breathe new life into the culture change initiative, which she began to lead with greater conviction and effectiveness. Her team noticed the change and followed her example by giving more of their discretionary energy to the effort. Two months later, the culture change effort was in full bloom, and Tina and her team became role models of the change effort for the rest of the organization.

Your Turn

1. Tina had a clear purpose for doing her work, which was to make a difference in the lives of others. What is your purpose at work?

2. Think about the last time you felt inspired. What were you doing? What challenges or opportunities did you face? Who else was involved?

3. Drawing on your responses to the preceding two questions, list the key sources of inspiration for you as a leader: those specific activities, events, or people that move you, ignite a feeling of possibility within you, or connect you with the life-giving force you need to create, innovate, and lead. Is it being in front of customers, listening to their concerns, and showing them how your services can help them? Is it problem solving with your team, learning about cutting-edge technology, or attending a collaborative strategy session with your peers? Which of your colleagues, friends, or family members have the capacity to inspire you, either with their words or their example?

If you've been disconnected from what enlivens you for any length of time, answering the preceding questions may have been a bit challenging for you. And even if you can answer them, your responses may be intellectual ones that live in your mind but not in your heart or your body. If this is the case, commit right now to reengaging in a new way with the activities, people, and sense of purpose that matter most to you. Take one small step today to do something that breathes new life into your leadership and build from there. Don't wait for a crisis to remind you of what you truly care about.

Leaders in particular run the risk of becoming disconnected from what they care about. It can be lonely at the top, and at times you will face tremendous inertia, daunting challenges, and disappointing setbacks. It's essential that you do whatever it takes to stay connected to what you care about most.

Phase 2: Envision Your Future

Once you've revived your own leadership, it's time to breathe new life into your organization by answering the question at the heart of this conversation: what's the better future you envision? Once you have that answer, you can communicate it to those whose support you need. Your vision must be clear and compelling—first and foremost to yourself, and then to those who must execute it. As you begin to articulate and communicate the future you want to create, your goal is to build a *shared understanding* so that the future is clear to everyone who will be a part of it.

In our work with leaders, we've found the following questions to be helpful in generating a vision or crystallizing one they may already have. As you read these questions, pause for a moment after each one. Are your answers clear? Compelling to you? Shared by others? Although the questions are simple, arriving at the answers to them isn't easy. Doing so requires a deep understanding of the challenges and opportunities your business or organization faces, along with time and space for reflection.

Questions for Envisioning a Better Future

1. What are we building here together?
2. Where are we headed, and why?
3. How will we (and others) be better off as result of creating this future?
4. How will we know when we're there?
5. What's our plan for getting there?

The future these questions will help you shape may be expressed in different ways depending on the role you play in your organization and the scope of leadership you exercise. For example, as a CEO, you might express your vision as an overarching aspiration ("To make the leap from being a good company to a great one") or as a set of specific strategic priorities ("launch new, innovative product lines in the next six months and increase market share by 10 percent in the next year"). As a team leader, your vision might take the form of a concrete goal that links to the broader organizational strategy and vision ("Create a state-of-the-art online learning platform that increases member retention and engagement," for example).

Regardless of the specific form or language you use to convey the future you want to create, provide your team with *clarity* about where you are leading them and a sense of *optimism* about getting there. Let's take a closer look at these two essential ingredients, each of which is like oxygen to your followers; without them, you cannot breathe new life into your organization.

Creating Organizational Clarity

Almost nothing impedes an organization's progress and stifles your team's best efforts as much as a lack of clarity. When leaders are not clear about the future they envision, why it matters, or the plan for getting there, teams will be ineffective and ultimately fail, no matter how hard thcy work.

To create organizational clarity as a leader, you will need to communicate the better future you envision—and your plan for getting there—with specificity and regularity. Once or twice is not enough. In fact, a good sign that you are communicating with enough frequency is when you start to sound like a broken record to yourself. Remember, you've probably been thinking about the future much longer than you've been speaking to others about it, so your memory and their memory of it aren't the same. Keep in mind that your goal here is to create *shared understanding* of where you are headed and why it matters, and this requires that you engage people in an ongoing two-way conversation. Sending out information via e-mail or simply having an occasional staff meeting that's a one-way presentation instead of a two-way dialogue isn't enough to build shared understanding.

Cultivating the Right Kind of Optimism

Being clear about where you are headed is vital, but your team must also feel optimistic about the future. If not, why would anyone want to go there, and what reasons would they have for working hard to make it happen?

Research conducted by Dr. Martin Seligman, a well-known psychologist and professor at the University of Pennsylvania, has shown that optimism contributes to happiness, well-being, *and* success. Optimistic people tend to respond better to adversity, have more confidence in their own abilities, and often achieve more than their pessimistic counterparts. Cultivating optimism in yourself and in those you lead is part of the process of inspiring others to create a better future.

But what if you weren't born an optimist? The good news is that you can learn to be more optimistic. In his groundbreaking book *Learned Optimism,* Seligman makes a convincing argument that anyone can learn to *think and behave* more optimistically—and, in doing so, improve her outcomes and quality of life.[1] The simple techniques Seligman has devised for learning optimism have since been tested and taught to a wide variety of people, including teachers, caregivers, business professionals, soldiers, and people suffering from depression. Several other studies have confirmed Seligman's findings that optimism can be learned, cultivated, and strengthened.

However, not just any kind of optimism will do when it comes to exercising leadership. In his book *Better under Pressure,* Justin Menkes reveals that leaders are most effective when they employ what's called *realistic optimism.*[2] Menkes defines realistic optimism as a combination of two characteristics: *personal agency,* which is a belief that your actions can and will influence outcomes, and *awareness of actual circumstances,* which means that a leader has a firm grasp of his current reality and the obstacles ahead. Menkes calls the latter piece of realistic optimism "seeing the world as it really is." The sense of personal agency empowers a leader to tackle challenges others find insurmountable while retaining a realistic view of how much hard work, perseverance, and ingenuity are required to succeed. In Menkes's eight-year study of CEOs who succeeded at the helm despite tough economic conditions, realistic optimism emerged as one of three attributes that separated the successful CEOs from those who faltered and ultimately failed.

Menkes's research reinforces similar findings published in 2001 by Jim Collins in his seminal book *Good to Great.* Collins wrote about the importance of leaders "facing the brutal facts" of their situation as one of the first steps in leading a company to greatness. According to Collins's research, those companies that were able to make the leap from good to great were more often led by people who displayed a duality of thinking that Collins termed the Stockdale Principle: "Retain absolute faith that you can and will prevail in the end, regardless of the difficulties, AND *at the same time* confront the most brutal facts of your current reality, whatever they might be."[3] The effect gets its name from Admiral Jim Stockdale, a high-ranking officer who endured a long and harrowing imprisonment in a Hanoi war camp during the Vietnam War. Stockdale managed to employ this dualistic thinking for more than eight years, until he was finally released at the end of the war.

Whether you call it realistic optimism or the Stockdale Principle, leaders who use this strategy build a shared understanding of the obstacles ahead along with the fortitude to deal with them. Their teams share a grounded hopefulness in their capacity to prevail.

To what extent do you possess realistic optimism? How grounded is your vision in the facts and realities of your situation? How do you know? We'll return to these questions later, but for now let's take a look at how one leader we coached benefited from realistic optimism.

The Right Dose of Optimism: Jim's Story

Jim reached out to us in part because he had begun to feel stale in his leadership and restless in his business. In our first meeting with him, Jim recounted the first six years of his company's existence and how he had led his team through many of the daunting challenges associated with a start-up. Now that things had stabilized, he found himself out of sorts and a bit disengaged. He liked the chase of winning new clients, but lately he had been spending most of his time in the office focusing on internal initiatives that, though important, bored him. He wanted to find a reason to participate more wholeheartedly in the life of his company. And even more important, Jim knew he needed to reenvision his business and set a compelling new direction for his team. Before he could do that, he needed a little inspiration of his own.

We suggested that Jim reengage with the people and things that inspired him. Jim felt most enlivened when he was meeting with clients, learning about their needs, and exploring how his company's services and products could help them. He'd moved away from client contact, and his energy and inspiration had suffered as result. Jim made a plan to visit several clients in the coming months.

We also asked him to name the core purpose of his work: "Building something of lasting value versus making a quick buck and a quick exit," he told us. He wanted to leave a legacy and a company that outlasted him. Jim realized he had to get back in the game of envisioning a new future or his company wouldn't survive. His business was facing a number of external challenges and changes in the marketplace. One of these realities—a declining demand for his main product line—was already impacting new sales. If Jim didn't figure out another way to compete, he knew his business would shrink and, eventually, die.

Jim was looking for new ideas to stimulate his thinking about his business, so we suggested that he read the book *Good to Great.* He agreed to and read it while he was flying to visit clients. When we met with him again a month later, Jim was energized and engaged in a way that he hadn't been when we first met with him. He'd found many of the ideas in the book helpful, and they had provided him with a new way to think about his business. His visits to clients had reinvigorated him and had given him the seeds of a new vision for the company. Jim was beginning to see that technology needed to play a much bigger role in the life of his business and in its core offerings.

Over the course of several weeks, Jim continued to reflect on what he thought his business was best at and what direction should be next. He also asked his management team to read *Good to Great* and engaged them in several discussions about the current realities they were facing and the future they wanted to create. He and his team ultimately ended up with a one-sentence statement that gave them a newfound sense of clarity, identity, and direction.

The dialogue that went into crafting this statement was robust and inclusive, and based in part on Jim's belief from his client visits that they could do far more with technology than they currently were. As a result, Jim's company invested heavily in a new technology platform and created new service offerings based on this platform.

During the inevitable ups and downs of forging a new direction for his company, Jim continued to stay the course and to express realistic optimism about the future. He regularly required that he and his team face the facts and the tough decisions in front of them, even when doing so was unpleasant and challenging; at the same time, he continued to express his complete confidence in his team's capacity to prevail and never wavered in his own commitment to make their desired future happen. Today, his company is enjoying the fruits of Jim's and his team's labor: renewed business, increased sales, and a thriving management team.

Your Turn

1. As you look ahead, do you see a better future for the organization, team, or project you are leading? If not, what will it take to envision one?

2. In the preceding story, Jim cared about creating a legacy and a company that outlasted him. For a vision to be compelling, it must be connected to what you and others care about. To what extent do you care about the future you are working to create? Why does it matter to you? To your customers? To your team?

3. Consider some of the "brutal facts" that you and your team must face if you are to succeed in creating the new future you envision. How can you speak the truth about these realities and the challenges that lie ahead while still fostering a sense of hope and optimism?

4. For Jim to succeed in creating a better future for his company, he needed to cultivate a more optimistic mind-set. For your vision to

succeed, will something new be required of you as a leader? If so, what is it?

As Jim envisioned where he wanted to lead his business, he reached out to his management team to get them involved. He wanted to create a shared understanding of his vision and cultivate the two essential ingredients of clarity and optimism. However, you'll recall that the goal of the Inspiration Conversation is to create a shared future. In addition to building a shared *understanding* of your vision, you must also build shared *commitment.* The final phase of the Inspiration Conversation will show you how.

Phase 3: Enroll Others in Advancing the Future

In 2010, the San Francisco 49ers were struggling and had been out of the NFL playoffs for years. A new coach, Jim Harbaugh, took over. In just two seasons he led the 49ers to the Super Bowl, with essentially the same players he inherited. How did he lead a team the league had dismissed as losers to the Super Bowl in such a short period of time? And what does his success reveal to us about how we can inspire our own teams and enroll them in the future we want to create?

As both a former player and a coach, Harbaugh brought a number of leadership qualities to the 49ers that were instrumental in their turnaround, including intensity, focus, passion, optimism, and deep knowledge of the game. He also connected well with players and genuinely cared about them. All of these attributes enabled him to provide a much-needed spark to a demoralized team. Jim Harbaugh had a bold vision, high standards, and a way of enrolling players in his cause that was masterful. One of the most powerful ways he did this was by sharing his own personal experiences and connecting them to the hopes and aspirations of his team.

Sportswriter Jeff Chadiha described how Harbaugh shared a personal anecdote with his players early in his tenure, and how it ended up becoming an inspiring team slogan.[4] When Jim and his siblings were young children living in humble circumstances, their family motto was, "Who's got it better than us?" They lived in tiny, cramped homes and traveled frequently to follow their father, Jack Harbaugh, from job to job as a college coach. Jack Harbaugh regularly gathered the family and asked enthusiastically, "Who's got it better than us?" The children would joyfully reply, "Nobody!" It wasn't until years later when he was an adult that Harbaugh realized that a *lot* of people had had it better than they (those houses they grew up in were *really* tiny). But he believed his father's message and learned a valuable lesson from it: you have everything you need right in front of you if you are willing to work hard, be resourceful, and believe in yourself and your family.

Harbaugh shared this personal story with his new team when they had only six weeks to get ready for the season, a losing record to overcome, and a host of critics who predicted they'd fail again. The story landed with his players and quickly took on a life of its own. It's now the team's motto. After practices and games, you can hear Harbaugh yelling, "Who's got it better than us?" His players yell back in unison, "Nobody!" The team motto is one of the ways Harbaugh keeps his players focused on the future.

While you may not be taking over a failing team, you must still speak about the future in a way that galvanizes your followers. It's one of four things we suggest leaders do to enroll others in advancing the future. As you read these suggestions, notice which feel easiest for you and which may need more of your time and attention:

1. *Find messages that resonate.* Like Harbaugh, you'll need to find your own key messages for your team. Anecdotes, metaphors, and slogans that resonate are what stir an emotional response in people.
2. *Develop a plan and continually refine it.* A vision without a plan is nothing more than a great idea. To advance your vision, you'll need to develop a thorough, rigorous plan *in collaboration with* those who will execute it. A well-crafted plan ensures that your vision isn't just wishful thinking that will be swept away by the tides of competing demands and distractions.
3. *Focus on the future.* Keeping the future front and center—for you and your team—is essential. This can be done by engaging regu-

larly in an ongoing dialogue with your team and other stakeholders around the plan you've developed, the progress you are making, and the obstacles that must be overcome along the way. Celebrating successes is also an essential part of keeping people focused and engaged.

4. *Keep it autonomous.* If you want your team members to bring their full commitment, you'll need to give them some latitude. Self-direction is a critical factor in employee engagement and productivity and is vital to the process of enrollment.

For some leaders and business owners we've coached, giving employees autonomy is a bit of a sticking point. This certainly was the case for our client, John. John liked to exercise total control over his business; finding ways to meaningfully involve his employees didn't always come easy to him. Let's see what he did to overcome his reluctance and propel his team and his business forward.

Learning to Let Go: John's Story

John ran a hugely successful dental practice that prided itself on extraordinary patient care and cutting-edge technology. But John felt that he and his team had reached a plateau, and he didn't know how to lead beyond it. He reached out to us to help him figure out how he might inspire his team to a new level of results. When we first met with John, he had already articulated a clear, overarching vision for the practice and had set a new goal for the team, which was to get 10 percent better in the year ahead. He was committed to this goal—but was his team?

We challenged John and his team to define what exactly they meant by 10 percent better. We asked them to identify three areas in the business where they most wanted to improve and helped the team identify some metrics for assessing their progress. They chose to focus on patient care, teamwork, and new client referrals. John was initially reluctant to involve his team in selecting these three areas. However, we explained that engaging his team would help them feel like the goal was something they had a stake in creating rather than something he was imposing on them.

Next, we helped John and his team craft a plan for how they would accomplish their goal. They decided that, each month, they would focus on one of the three target areas they had selected for improvement, starting with patient care. At the beginning of each day, they would ask themselves, "What's one small step I can take today to improve patient care?" They agreed to take action on whatever ideas came to them and to notice the difference their actions made. They also agreed to record all their ideas and share them with the rest of the team at the end of the month.

At our next meeting, everyone shared the small steps they had taken to improve patient care. It was a robust and engaging meeting, and everyone appeared genuinely committed to the cause and encouraged by some of their early wins. For the next month, they picked one of their other targeted areas and repeated this process until they had cycled through all three areas. Over the course of three months, the team implemented several new patient care practices and improved existing ones, strengthened team communication and collaboration, and refined their process for gaining new client referrals. They also grew increasingly confident in, and committed to, the goal of getting 10 percent better, which was no longer just John's goal but theirs as well.

When we met with John and his team for a final time, his team members shared their new team vision, which they had developed jointly: "We are committed to being a superstar team who provides extraordinary patient care." They also had a new team slogan: "We are the Starbucks of Dentistry." It captured their aspirations in a simple yet compelling way: happy patients, repeat customers, a commitment to excellence, and brand recognition in their industry. Because the team frequently visited Starbucks on their breaks, each visit reminded them of their slogan, which in turn reminded them of their commitment and vision.

John's vision of getting 10 percent better was now something the team fully embraced. As the year unfolded, the team continued to focus each month on their goal, and to John's delight, they brought a new level of commitment and ownership to achieving it.

Your Turn

Take a few minutes to reflect on the degree to which you have enrolled your team members in the better future you envision. To what extent has *your* vision become *theirs*? Use the following questions as a guide:

1. John's team members became more invested and engaged in his vision when he involved them and gave them a meaningful role in making it happen. To what extent have you involved your team members in shaping your vision and in figuring out how best to achieve it? How or where might you give them more autonomy or latitude to do so?

2. John and his team developed an ongoing monthly process that kept them focused on the vision and their progress. Do you have a process in place that keeps your team focused on the future you want to create? If not, what steps might you take to change that?

3. If we were to ask your team members what they think your vision is, what might they say? How close would their answers mirror your own? If the answer is, "I'm not sure," you have some work to do in creating a shared understanding of your vision and a shared commitment to advancing it. What steps might you take this week to accomplish that?

How Important Is Autonomy to Enrollment?

Giving employees at least some autonomy in how they execute your vision of the future is one of the four suggestions we mentioned earlier for enrolling others in your cause. But how important is autonomy, and what does the research have to say about it?

According to best-selling author Daniel Pink, autonomy is one of three factors that science shows leads to better performance (the other two being mastery and a sense of purpose). Autonomy refers to our drive as humans to be self-directed and to have a say in the course of our day, our careers, and our lives. In his book *Drive,* Pink cites several research studies that show the link between autonomy and performance.[5] When employees are given more latitude around choosing what they work on, when they work, and with whom they work, they are more creative, productive, and engaged. They are also more innovative. One business that has chosen to act on this finding is the Australian company Atlassian. Once a quarter, their software developers can spend twenty-four hours working on whatever projects or tasks they want, with whomever they want, and wherever they want. The only stipulation is that they must share their results and what they learned at a joint meeting with other developers. This quarterly ritual has resulted in a number of ideas for new products and has given rise to numerous software fixes, solutions, and improvements. One day of autonomy each quarter has unleashed an impressive bounty of creativity and innovation.

Pink cites several other studies and real-life examples to support the claim that autonomy is a key motivator and driver of performance. If you think about your own experience, this is probably true for you. When you are given the latitude to figure out how best to do something on your own, don't you feel more engaged, creative, and committed? Human beings are wired to create and innovate.

What does this have to do with you? If all you want as a leader is for people to comply with your vision, the answer might be "nothing." However, if you want people to bring their best efforts and discretionary energy to advancing your cause, you'll have to engage their hearts and their minds in the process—which means giving them a voice and a choice in what, when, and how things happen. Along with organizational clarity and realistic optimism, autonomy is a key ingredient of a vibrant organization.

Dealing with Resistance and Sabotage

We mentioned earlier how all living systems naturally work to preserve and protect the status quo. This is true of biological systems like the human body and it's also true of institutions and teams. To some extent, this is healthy, but it can also work against you. As you lead people in the creation of a new future, you will be challenging the status quo. Even if it's a future that people find compelling, parts of the system will work against you to restore the old order of things in the form of resistance and, in some cases, even sabotage. As Edwin Friedman, leadership theorist and author, noted, "sabotage is not merely something to be avoided or wished away; instead it comes with the territory of leading, whether that territory is a family or an organization."[6] In fact, Friedman believed that a leader's capacity and willingness to deal with sabotage are the defining factors of success.

The bigger the change and the bolder your vision, the greater the resistance you are likely to face. It's one more reason why you need to regularly connect with what inspires you and what breathes new life into your work. Otherwise, you won't have the capacity you need to stay the course under pressure. Exactly *how* you deal with this inevitable resistance and sabotage is key, but before we talk about that, let's explore a bit more what we mean by resistance and sabotage.

Resistance can come in many guises. Sometimes it takes the form of defending old ways ("But we've always done it this way!") or simply dragging feet on a project or initiative. Sometimes it shows up as pessimism ("This will never work here") or fear and self-doubt ("I don't think we can handle this").

Sabotage is an extreme form of resistance. Here, people aren't just resisting the change or vision you've put forth; they are working to *undermine* it, either directly or indirectly. Sometimes their undermining takes the form of backdoor conversations and shifting alliances; at other times, it's more direct and straightforward—for example, when a colleague publicly expresses dislike of your vision (or your leadership) in a way that catches you off guard and derails your plan.

Here are a few guidelines we've shared with our coaching clients on how to deal effectively with resistance and sabotage. Which of these might you be able to incorporate into your own leadership repertoire?

1. *Face and embrace the resistance.* Face resistance head-on by expecting it, recognizing it for what it is (a natural response to change), and resolving to do something about it in a thoughtful and deliberate way.

When you determine that there is some resistance to the changes you are trying to make, it's often better to get it out in the open by letting people have a time and place to express their concerns, complaints, or fears. We heard a saying once that describes the balance you want to strike here: "You can let people visit pity city, but don't let them park there!" Allow for some venting and questioning to be openly expressed, yet reinforce some limits. It's like letting the steam escape from a boiling pot of water, but without removing the entire lid. Keeping the lid on tight with the heat on high, conversely, results in the water spilling over. Knowing when to lift the lid enough to let some of the steam escape (and when to turn down the heat if necessary) is part of the artful dance in which leaders must engage as they move people into a new and uncertain future.

2. *Don't take it so personally.* Resistance to you or to your vision can feel like a personal attack instead of what it is: a systemic and natural reaction to change. So while it might feel personal, remind yourself that it's not. Doing so will help you to maintain some much-needed perspective as you manage the ups and downs of leading change.

3. *Stay connected to your saboteurs.* It can be easy to slip into an avoidance pattern with team members who push back. Instead, work to stay connected to these individuals without letting them hijack your agenda or your energy. Occasionally reach out to them, engaging in open dialogue with them while at the same time holding your ground. Although you don't have to necessarily win them over, you do need to stay connected. Doing so minimizes their ability to rally others to their side and demonstrates your capacity for facing conflict and disagreement, while at the same time staying the course.

4. *Distinguish between productive and reactive complaints.* The former are worth your time and energy; the latter aren't. How do you know which is which? As we discussed in the Capacity Conversation, a productive complaint is one that is delivered at the right time, to the right person, in the right place, and with the right tone or mood. Listen to these and encourage them. Some you may agree with; others you may not. Either way, listening openly to others who are thoughtful with their complaints will go a long way toward enrolling them in your cause. Reactive complaints,

conversely, are gripes, problems, or issues that aren't delivered thoughtfully or with care. Often they are delivered to the wrong person (someone other than the person who can actually do something about it) and usually stem from people feeling anxious and wanting to vent. Again, see them for what they are, and don't allow reactive complaints to hijack your time and energy.

5. *Stay the course.* When you are hit with the full force of resistance or sabotage, it can throw you off your game and make you waver in your commitment and resolve. This is only natural, yet you must continue to move forward even in the face of your own self-doubt and weariness. If you know in your heart and mind that the course you have set for your team or organization is the right one, then as the saying goes, you must "keep calm and carry on."

The Inspiration Conversation: Key Takeaways

All systems and organizations naturally want to preserve the status quo. Your job as a leader is to imagine a future that lies beyond that and to rally others to achieve it. Before you can do that, however, you need to breathe new life into your own leadership. This chapter began with an invitation for you to reconnect with the people, projects, and sense of purpose that enliven you. With a renewed sense of purpose, you thoughtfully reflected on the core question posed in this chapter: "What's the better future I can see?" As a result, you may have landed on a new vision, goal, or direction for your organization or recommitted to an existing one that needs your attention. Either way, you're now poised to enroll others in your cause by building a *shared* understanding of where you are headed, why it matters, and how you'll get there. Once your team has had a voice in creating your shared future, they'll be more committed to making it happen.

Along the way, you will likely encounter resistance, and maybe even sabotage, as the system works to protect the status quo. Plan to skillfully stay the course by grounding yourself in realistic optimism and staying connected—not only to your sense of purpose but also to those who may not fully support your vision or your plans. As you engage in the Inspiration Conversation you will discover a renewed commitment to lead, along with a shared future that people care about.

The Inspiration Conversation: What's Next?

Coaching Assignments for Leveraging Your Learning

Is the Inspiration Conversation particularly critical for you? The following list of Actions, Practices, and Resources is a tool kit for engaging more deeply in this important Missing Conversation.

Action Steps

- Find out how clear your team is about the future you want to create. At your next staff meeting or as part of your one-on-one status meetings with employees, ask them, "Where do *you* think we are headed as an organization?" Listen closely to their responses and then share with them your own. Use this as an opportunity to build shared understanding and alignment around your vision.
- If you've found through reading this chapter that your vision for the future is unclear, set aside some time in your calendar to reflect, to gather information, and to engage with others to get clear. Make this one of your top priorities.
- Review your list of the specific activities and people that breathe new life into your leadership (see page 146). Pick one or two and commit to reconnecting with one of these activities or people this week.
- Think of a metaphor, visual image, or story you might use to evoke the future you want to create. Try it out on someone to see how it lands, and then refine it if necessary. Use it the next time you speak about your vision to help others better understand why it matters to you and the role they can play in making it happen.

Ongoing Practices

- Do you have a regular, recurring meeting with your team that is devoted to discussing the future, your progress toward creating it, and the next steps needed? If not, create a schedule—monthly or bimonthly—*and stick to it.*
- Find a way to acknowledge and celebrate wins on a regular basis. This can be done as part of your regularly scheduled meetings, in a separate e-mail that you send out periodically, or both. Keeping people focused on wins helps to build the realistic optimism that is so essential to your success.

Suggested Resources

Better under Pressure: How Great Leaders Bring Out the Best in Themselves and Others by Justin Menkes: Harvard Business Review Press, 2011.

Good to Great: Why Some Companies Make the Leap . . . and Others Don't by Jim Collins: HarperCollins, 2001.

The Leader's Guide to Storytelling: Mastering the Art and Discipline of Business Narrative by Stephen Denning: John Wiley, 2011.

The One Thing You Need to Know: About Great Managing, Great Leadership, and Sustained Individual Success by Marcus Buckingham: Free Press, 2005.

Resilient Leadership: Navigating the Hidden Chemistry of Organizations by Bob Duggan and Jim Moyer: Infinity, 2009.

CHAPTER 8

Where Is My Attention Going? The Strategic Focus Conversation

Whatever we pay attention to powerfully and consistently will always grow larger in our lives.

—**Adrian Savage,** *A Spark from Heaven*

When was the last time you stopped to really think about where your attention is going—and, just as important, where it's not?

The ability to choose where you place your attention is one of your most powerful gifts. Your attention is like an inner spotlight that you can shine in any direction: outward toward your surrounding environment or inward toward your thoughts, feelings, and sensations.

Take a moment right now to exercise this choice. First, shine the spotlight of your attention on the words you are reading. Now, direct your attention to the book you are holding and notice how it feels in your hands. How heavy is it? What does its texture feel like? Now, focus your attention on the sounds around you. Pause for a moment to really notice and take in what you hear. Finally, bring your attention back to your hands and to the book you are holding. Your attention is an incredibly powerful instrument—and you can choose both where to direct it and the quality of focus you bring to what you encounter in your daily life.

While this innate capacity is part of your human endowment, it is under siege by the blistering pace and 24/7 connectivity of modern life. If you're like many of the leaders with whom we work, you're bombarded daily by a never-ending stream of incoming possibilities, demands, and distractions, which can hijack your attention without your awareness or explicit consent.

The end result is that you can spend too many of your days flitting from one task, idea, or challenge to the next, without ever really bringing your focused attention and best thinking to any of them. When this happens, you can begin to feel like you're a full-time firefighter constantly reacting to the crisis of the day: increasingly busy yet feeling less and less productive, engaged, and energized.

In this chapter, we invite you to step into the Strategic Focus Conversation.

The reflections and practices that make up this conversation are a powerful antidote to the scattered, fragmented, never-feeling-quite-on-top-of-it existence many leaders experience on a daily basis—an existence that not only dilutes your effectiveness but robs you of the kind of satisfaction and fulfillment that come from deeply immersing yourself in an activity and bringing your full engagement.

If you'd like to deploy your attention in a more strategic and focused way, read on. We'll walk you through the three phases of the Strategic Focus Conversation and give you a mastery tool kit that will allow you to refocus your attention where it's needed most.

Phase 1: Pay Attention to How You're Paying Attention

Your Strategic Focus Conversation begins by noticing how you're paying attention: observing in the moment what gets your attention; what hijacks it; and whether the quality of attention you're giving to your work is producing the results you desire.

You may discover that, like many modern-day leaders, you've lost the fine art of focusing.

In her book *Distracted,* Maggie Jackson cites one yearlong study that found that workers switch tasks every three minutes; nearly half the time, they interrupt themselves. In another study she cites, nearly a third of employees said they often don't have time to reflect on or process the work they do, let alone think about their future.[1]

Many knowledge workers live and work in a state that Linda Stone, a writer and consultant, calls *continuous partial attention.*[2] It refers to a mode of attention where you're on constant alert, always plugged in to your networks of connectivity and constantly scanning them for opportunities. Though this mode is helpful in small doses, as a primary form of paying attention, it can produce an artificial sense of constant crisis. Over time, continuous partial attention can lead to a stressful lifestyle and dilute your ability to reflect, to be decisive, and to think creatively.

Unlike continuous partial attention, multitasking is about being more productive and efficient. Eating dinner while you read a report, doing the dishes while you talk on the phone to a friend, or filing papers while you listen to phone messages are simple ways you might try to accomplish more in less time.

For the most part, these simpler forms of multitasking seem to work for us. However, research conducted by psychologist David Meyer at the University of Michigan suggests that multitasking is less valuable when it involves more substantive cognitive tasks.[3] A closer look at how the brain works reveals that humans aren't capable of actually focusing on and thinking about two or more things simultaneously. Rather, when you multitask, you're switching gears mentally as you flip back and forth between tasks. So although you might think you're handling more than one thing at a time, in actuality, you're not.

According to Meyers, the cost of this mental switching can be substantial. It turns out that constant multitasking is mentally depleting and that you become increasingly fatigued from shifting your focus repeatedly between two or more tasks. In addition, multitasking contributes to the release of stress hormones and adrenaline, which can cause long-term health problems and contribute to the loss of short-term memory.[4]

The bottom line? How you pay attention has profound implications for your leadership and life. This was certainly the case for John, a recently promoted director with whom we worked. Let's look at his story to see how he chose to engage in the Strategic Focus Conversation.

Adjusting Focus: John's Story

Shortly after John's promotion to director of his high-tech company, he opted to participate in an executive coaching initiative his manager launched with his entire leadership team. We were brought in to support the initiative. John came to coaching with two goals: to improve his communication skills with key stakeholders and to figure out how to bring greater focus to his work.

We asked John to identify the things that hijacked his attention on a regular basis. We explained that an "attention hijacker" was anything that diverted or derailed his attention *without his full awareness or explicit consent.* We also asked him to notice when he was bringing his best thinking and full attention to an activity at work and, conversely, when he wasn't.

John was most frustrated by the steady stream of back-to-back internal meetings in which he participated on a regular basis. Many of these meetings were scheduled by other people—frequently at the last minute. John noticed that he was inattentive and resentful at these meetings, which drained his energy and made him feel frustrated and unproductive.

He also noticed that he felt like he wasn't bringing his best thinking or full attention to much of anything at work, with the exception of client meetings. With clients, John was fully focused, attentive, and creative. When we asked him what was different about client meetings, he identified three things: (1) Every client meeting had a clear focus, (2) the purpose of those meetings mattered to him, and (3) he always did his homework and was well prepared.

John realized that these three elements were the missing ingredients in the frustrating internal meetings. He felt he couldn't opt out of these meetings, but he *could* change the way he paid attention in them. John committed to finding out in advance the purpose of each internal meeting and the role he was expected to play. He also identified a clear focus for himself. Many times this purpose wasn't directly related to the agenda of the meeting but instead centered on building greater visibility and connection with key stakeholders. During these meetings, John practiced paying attention to how he listened (or didn't) and to the level of engagement and openness he conveyed.

Over time, John began to show up quite differently in these meetings, and this made all the difference. What was once a frustrating distraction that depleted his energy and diluted his attention became an opportunity to engage, connect, and learn. His renewed commitment had the added benefit of improving his rapport and connection with key stakeholders and opened the door for more strategic dialogue.

Your Turn

Where is your attention going these days, and how is this defining the quality of your leadership and life? Take a few minutes to delve a bit more deeply into this inquiry by reflecting on the following questions:

1. What are your biggest distractions and attention hijackers right now? How might you begin to deal with these more proactively?

2. Which activities at work receive your full attention and best thinking on a regular basis? Which ones do not? How does this affect your satisfaction and effectiveness?

3. To what extent do you employ continuous partial attention and multitasking on a daily basis? In what way are these modes of attending serving you? In what ways might they be getting in your way?

Sometimes changing just one attention-diluting habit can make all the difference. To see how, let's take a look at the story of Mark, an executive consultant who came to us for help.

Curbing E-mail Mania: Mark's Story

Mark was a successful executive who came to us because he felt overwhelmed by his company's rapid growth and he knew his followers were finding his leadership chaotic and unfocused. When we first met with Mark, we asked him to think about where his employees needed more clarity and direction and how he might begin to provide it. We also helped him identify the specific projects and priorities that needed more of his best thinking and focused attention.

As Mark began to pay more attention to how he was paying attention, he realized that one of his biggest attention hijackers was e-mail. He began most mornings by checking his Blackberry and immediately firing off a number of quick responses to e-mails before he had eaten breakfast or even thought about what he wanted to accomplish that day. He was often drawn into responding to e-mails that weren't really important, and this habit meant he started his day on a reactive rather than a proactive note.

Once at the office, he checked his e-mail whenever he could, trying in vain to get through it efficiently. He constantly felt behind, certain that important messages were falling through the cracks. Mark just couldn't seem to get on top of his inbox—and he had a backlog of more than three thousand unread messages. After engaging in the Strategic Focus Conversation, Mark began a new practice around how he handled his e-mail—one that produced big dividends.

He decided he would check and respond to e-mails four times a day: early morning, midday, an hour or so before he left the office, and once in the evening after dinner. During the morning and midday periods, he would respond only to those items that were important and urgent; he put all other messages in one of several inbox folders he created. In the late afternoon, he would go back and respond thoughtfully to the earlier messages he had filed and do some additional responding to new messages as needed. Once he was home for the evening, he resolved to check his e-mail only once for any urgent matters. He also went through the backlog of messages in his inbox, deleted most of them, and filed the rest.

This simple practice gave Mark more breathing room and cleared out some of the mental debris that cluttered his thinking. With a bit more mental space and longer pockets of undistracted time, Mark was able to more fully focus on the strategic issues and challenges he faced. This new practice had the added benefit of removing a major stressor and energy drainer in his day.

Your Turn

1. Reflect on how you currently handle e-mail. The sheer volume of it proves to be an overwhelming distraction for many of the leaders we coach. Do you have an effective system in place for responding to e-mail? If not, what changes might you make?

2. Which of the following *attention-diluting habits* do you see in yourself, and in what way might they be sabotaging you? Pick one that most undermines your effectiveness and resolve to change it this week.

Attention-Diluting Habits

- Starting your day by checking and reacting to e-mails
- Multitasking regularly with two or more cognitive tasks (e.g., listening to a conference call while responding to e-mails), each of which requires your full attention to do well
- Constantly checking your phone during the day, even while in meetings or when walking through the office
- Working long hours without taking any breaks to clear your mind
- Allowing drop-ins and requests from employees and colleagues to repeatedly divert your attention from the projects or priorities you most want to advance

As you continue to *pay attention to how you're paying attention,* you can see more clearly how your habits of attention work for and against you, and this opens up new possibilities for choice.

However, it's important to note that your end goal is not to become completely focused at all times. This is unrealistic given the environments in which we work and the way our brains are wired. And in fact, it's not even desirable. As you'll see later in this chapter, having space in your week for your mind to wander freely can lead to flashes of insight and greater creativity.

Rather than striving to be focused at all times, your goal is to become more *intentional* about your attention—to choose with greater discernment *when* you pay attention, *how* you pay attention, and *what* you pay attention to. Phase 2 of the Strategic Focus Conversation deals with that "what."

PHASE 2: CONSCIOUSLY DIRECT YOUR ATTENTION

Bringing awareness to how you are attending wakes you up out of automatic pilot and into the present moment. You can see more clearly whether the way you're paying attention is producing the results you want. But awareness alone is not enough. To consciously choose your focus requires not only awareness but also two other essential ingredients:

- Clarity about your most important priorities
- The discipline and resolve to stay focused on them despite the competing demands on your time

Making a conscious choice to take charge of your attention and to focus on what matters most is one of the most important acts of leadership.

How do you choose what you will focus your attention on each day? Each week? Each year? From the many things to which you could attend, how do you differentiate the "vital few" from the "trivial many?"

Lessons from Those Who Fly

Years ago, we were at dinner with a seasoned executive and friend of ours, Paul, who was the leader of an eight-thousand-person organization.

We noticed that, unlike many of his peers in the same organization, Paul was unusually attentive, crystal-clear about his priorities (both professionally and personally), and consistently able to focus on them despite the competing demands on his time. Curious, we asked him why he thought this was the case and what he did to accomplish it.

He told us about something he'd learned years ago from a friend who was a pilot. Paul asked his friend how he managed to keep his focus when he was flying despite the complex display of dials, instruments, and indicators on a plane's display panel.

"It's simpler than you might think," the pilot responded. "We are taught which of these dials and indicators are most critical to keeping the plane flying properly and which aren't, and we focus only on a handful that make the critical difference. The rest we don't pay attention to unless circumstances arise that require us to, which is rare."

Paul explained to us that this simple story and the lesson embedded in it had always stayed with him. "I am always asking myself and my team what matters most, and then I vigilantly keep myself and others focused on those vital few priorities, along with a handful of indicators that tell us how we're doing." A few years later, Paul launched a company-wide initiative called "The Vital Few." The leaders in his organization, in partnership with their teams, aligned around a critical few priorities and were held accountable for keeping themselves and their employees focused.

Consciously choosing the "vital few" issues that need your focus on a daily, weekly, and yearly basis is essential to moving out of the space of a reactive manager and into the space of a strategic leader.

Dianne is of one of several clients with whom we have worked who successfully made this transition. As you read her story, notice what changes she made to take better charge of her attention and whether any of these shifts resonate with you.

Naming the Vital Few: Dianne's Story

Dianne was returning from maternity leave after taking four months off to have her second child. Upon returning to work, she was given the opportunity to work with us to prepare for an expanded role in her company.

Previously, Dianne had functioned largely as a subject matter expert who managed a small team. Now she was being asked to launch a brand-new, highly visible organization with twenty employees. This was an opportunity for her to be "an internal entrepreneur" of sorts, and she was both excited and a bit anxious. She knew that this new role would require her to deploy her attention very differently and that she would need to move away from the hands-on client work she had excelled at.

We coached her to think through exactly how she needed to shift her attention and encouraged her to distill her priorities into three main areas of focus. Her "vital few" priorities were:

- Developing and refining a strategic plan for her new organization and selling that plan internally
- Building new relationships with key stakeholders and engaging in dialogue with them about their needs and aspirations
- Building and structuring her new organization

Dianne also decided to start each day with a few minutes of quiet time to plan and prioritize. Not being one for extensive planning tools or routines, she chose three simple questions to ask herself each morning before she launched into her day: (1) What's important about today? (2) What's important about the week ahead? and (3) What must get done? These simple questions grounded her in a more proactive mind-set and acted as a compass to better navigate her hectic days.

Initially, Dianne struggled to keep her focus on her vital few priorities. Her environment continued to be difficult to manage, and the new habit of focusing her attention was challenging to develop. However, with persistence and commitment, she got better at shifting her attention back to her vital few priorities when she found herself slipping. In a few short months, Dianne was spending the majority of her time, energy, and attention on the priorities she identified and was enjoying the challenges and opportunities that her new role afforded her.

Your Turn

Take a few minutes to dive into this part of the Strategic Focus Conversation. Use the following questions as a guide:

1. Strategic focus requires space in your day to think, plan, and pause. To what extent are your days jam-packed, with little or no space to deal with the unexpected or to catch your breath? How might you begin to change this?

2. How do you determine what to give your attention to on a daily, weekly, or yearly basis? Do you have a planning and prioritizing process in place that works for you?

3. Identify what you believe to be your three most important strategic priorities for the next several months. Are they clear to you right now? If not, what do you need to do to get clearer about your "vital few"?

Phase 3: Access Your Best Thinking

Most of us carve out too little time to think, dream, experiment, ponder, or plan. We may not fully appreciate the consequences of this tendency. Psychologist Dr. Edward Hallowell powerfully articulates the link between thinking and innovation in his book *CrazyBusy*: "What separates the great innovator from the mere data gatherer is the ability to stop and think about what has been gathered."[5]

As a leader, you're called not just to take action but also to strategize, envision, and innovate. To do so, you need blocks of uninterrupted time when you can delve deeply into the issues and opportunities you face, experiment with different ways of looking at them, and develop new insights for resolving them. Being strategically focused means *bringing your best thinking and your full attention to the projects, priorities, and initiatives that matter most.* When and where do you do your best thinking? How might you begin to do more of it?

This was the question we explored with Susan and Brian, two leaders we coached who managed to find fresh answers to this inquiry. Each of their stories illustrates the value of two different modes of thinking.

1. *Deep-dive thinking.* Time you spend deeply immersed in your work, fully focused and fully absorbed for a sustained period of time
2. *Subconscious creative thinking.* Time you allow your mind to wander, to explore, and to make connections, usually while engaged in another activity that relaxes your conscious mind and creates space for new insights to occur

As you read their stories, consider which type of thinking you'd like to be doing more of, and how it might benefit your leadership and life if you did.

Deep-Dive Thinking: Brian's Story

Brian, a partner at a large law firm, was pulled all day long by various competing demands that consumed his time and attention. One of his biggest concerns was to figure out how he might provide greater strategic vision and direction for the new case he was leading.

Despite his best efforts, Brian wasn't succeeding. He found himself so busy just meeting daily demands that there was no time left over to develop a strategic vision for his case. When we asked Brian where he did his best thinking, he said it was not at the office, where he was repeatedly interrupted by colleagues, and it was definitely not at home, where his two young children vied for his attention.

When Brian could work from a Starbucks close to home, however, he managed to get some of his best work done. He agreed to set aside two full days on his calendar that month to work there and to immerse himself in his case. His goal was to use this time to develop the overall strategy for the case and a game plan for winning it.

When we met with him a few weeks later, Brian shared his experience with us. The days he had set aside for thinking and strategizing had been hijacked by an urgent client demand and a backlog of critical e-mails. Not wanting to disappoint us (or his team), Brian found another two days in his calendar and spent them at Starbucks, deeply immersed in his case. He emerged with an overall strategy that he felt good about, which he shared with his team.

Brian's biggest win was not the strategy he devised but something else instead: the time he had spent deeply immersed in his work had reconnected him to what he loved about being a lawyer. Bringing his full attention and his best thinking for a sustained period of time to the case revitalized him and reminded him of why he had gotten into the profession in the first place. His deep-dive thinking strategy had been so successful that Brian decided to make it a monthly practice. Brian resolved to spend one day a month away from the office, thinking deeply and without distraction about the legal challenges his client faced and how he and his team might overcome them.

Brian's story reminds us that there is more at stake than we might realize when we allow our attention to be repeatedly hijacked and diverted. After spending time in deep-dive thinking for the first time in many months, Brian emerged reinvigorated and reconnected to what he loved best about his work. Recent research supports Brian's experience and seems to indicate that not only are we more productive when we focus for periods of uninterrupted time; we are also happier.

Creative Thinking: Susan's Story

Susan's role as the leader of a 350-person organization required her to think and act strategically and to provide vision and direction to the various branches and teams in her organization. But as she said, "There's no time to think! We just put out fires all day."

Susan's only time to think and to give focused attention to the various initiatives on her plate was late at night, after she finished taking care of her responsibilities on the home front. It was difficult to do her best thinking late at night, after a long day of meetings and an evening spent taking care of her family.

As we began to explore with her how she might find more time in her already crowded day to think and strategize, we recalled that Susan was in the middle of training for a marathon. When asked if she found her daily running routines to be fertile ground for thinking and idea generation, she said that yes, in fact, she often found her mind working through various issues when she trained. Because this was something to which she was already committed, we decided to capitalize on it and helped her figure out how she could make it a more potent time.

She began to use a notebook to capture the issues and challenges she knew she needed to be pondering on a more regular basis. Before each run, she looked at her list and picked one thing to mull over while she ran. When she came back from her run, she'd note in the notebook any insights she had gained.

When we saw her again, she talked about how the practice was helping her to think through several critical conversations she needed to have but had been putting off. On one of her runs that week, she had gotten a sudden flash of insight about how best to approach one of these conversations—a much-needed talk with a colleague who was undermining one of her team's projects—along with the precise language for starting it. Having found the right words to express her concerns, she felt empowered to confront the issue.

Your Turn

Now that you have read Brian's and Susan's stories, pause for a moment to reflect on when and where you do your best thinking and how you might find new ways to do more of it:

1. When was the last time you did a "deep dive" with your attention? What did it feel like? What prevents you from doing this more often?

2. Think back to the last time a new idea, insight, or solution popped into your mind. Where were you, and what were you doing? How might you incorporate more of this kind of productive daydreaming into your week?

As leaders, we are frequently caught up in the doing of our work and sometimes forget how important it is to our success *and* satisfaction to think about, reflect on, and process our work. This vital time spent thinking is what allows us to infuse what we do with greater creativity, clarity, and care.

The Strategic Focus Conversation: Key Takeaways

As Hans Margolius wrote, "only in quiet waters do things mirror themselves undistorted." As you engaged in the Strategic Focus Conversation, you began to see more clearly where your attention is going and, just as important, where it's not. You stepped back from your daily demands to notice what hijacks your attention and how you might begin to deploy it more skillfully and wisely. You've become clearer about your vital few priorities and explored new ways to create more space in your day to think, strategize, and imagine. As you continue to pay attention to *how you're paying attention* and course correct when needed, you shift your mind-set from a reactive manager to a strategic leader and pave the way for those around you to do the same.

The Strategic Focus Conversation: What's Next?

Coaching Assignments for Leveraging Your Learning

Is the Strategic Focus Conversation particularly critical for you? The following list of Actions, Practices, and Resources is a tool kit for engaging more deeply in this important Missing Conversation.

Action Steps

- Experiment with working from home, from a Starbucks, or from any location where you can work uninterrupted, one day a week or every other week. Notice whether this helps you to bring more clarity and focus to your work. Notice also if this enhances your satisfaction.
- Connect with two or three key stakeholders in your organization and engage in a strategic dialogue. Where do they see your business or organization going? What issues or concerns are they grappling with, and how might their thinking inform yours?

- If you didn't already do this, spend some time identifying your "vital few" organizational or strategic priorities (see page 175). Then share these with your team of direct reports and ask them to share theirs with you.
- Is there a project, important decision, or initiative that is languishing because you have not been able to bring your best thinking and focused attention to it? If so, schedule a block of uninterrupted time to focus on it, and then keep your resolve to do so no matter what.

Ongoing Practices

- Twice a day, stop and take a moment to ask yourself, "Where is my attention going?" Notice both the quality and focus of your attention. Course correct as needed.
- *E-mail apnea,* another term coined by Linda Stone, refers to the tendency many of us have to hold our breath or to tense our bodies when checking e-mail.[6] Make it a regular practice to breathe more deeply and to relax stored tension when responding to e-mail.
- Consider taking a daily walk or short stroll to settle your mind and to create mental space for new ideas to occur.
- Reflect on the way you start your day and whether it helps or hinders your efforts to lead clearly and effectively. Do you jump into your day reactively, by reviewing e-mails or rushing to meetings, before you've had any time to plan, prioritize, or gather yourself? If so, experiment with a different morning routine, one that supports you being strategically focused, intentional, and clear.

Suggested Resources

Becoming a Strategic Leader: Your Role in Your Organization's Enduring Success by Richard L. Hughes and Katherine Colarelli Beatty: John Wiley, 2005.

CrazyBusy: Overstretched, Overbooked, and About to Snap! Strategies for Handling Your Fast-Paced Life by Edward M. Hallowell, MD: Ballantine Books, 2007.

Distracted: The Erosion of Attention and the Coming Dark Age by Maggie Jackson: Prometheus Books, 2009.

Focus: The Hidden Driver of Excellence by Daniel Goleman: HarperCollins, 2013.

CHAPTER 9

How Well Connected Am I to Those Around Me? The Relationship Conversation

A leader is someone who gets things done through other people.

—Warren Buffett

This final missing conversation reminds us that no matter how inspired our leadership vision may be or how well we focus on implementing it, our efforts will only succeed if people want to follow our lead. Our success hinges on whether we build the kinds of relationships that motivate others to join us and move our vision forward.

Whether you're a leader in a corporate, nonprofit, or government agency, you already understand the critical role customer or stakeholder relationships play in an organization's success. Entire departments are created to manage external relationships and customer service. But it's your network of internal relationships that influences the quality of your organization's external relationships. Productive internal relationships produce satisfied customers and supportive stakeholders for your organization.

Without a web of reliable connections within an organization, a leadership vision won't take root and deliverables can't be achieved. As James Kouzes and Barry Posner point out in their book *The Leadership Challenge*, "to get extraordinary things done, people have to rely on each other."[1] A damaged or distant relationship between you and another player in your organization can undermine the most well-conceived plan and sabotage your organization's success. Conversely, an organization that fosters trusting relationships can outperform low-trust organizations by up to 300 percent, as documented in a 2002 Watson Wyatt research report.

Pause for a moment to consider the time and energy you devote to internal relationship building. When was the last time you invited one of your direct reports to lunch and asked him about himself? How recently did you stop by one of your team member's offices to check in and genuinely connect with her? Does the percentage of your time that you spend attending to your relationships inside and outside of work match how essential these relationships are to you and your organization's success?

You're only leading if you have followers lined up behind or beside you ready to move your priorities forward. In a valiant effort to meet expectations and deadlines, many leaders we coach slip into the trance of execution, focusing their attention almost exclusively on taking action. Pressed for time, they lose sight of their relationship-building agenda and are surprised and confused when stakeholders resist their recommendations and requests. What they most want is engagement and support from team members, but what they experience instead is reluctant compliance.

Trance of Execution

What do we mean by the trance of execution? Like many leaders we know, your energy and attention may become almost exclusively focused on taking action and achieving deliverables, and your conversations with others at work become transactional: who needs to do what by when? People around you become identified by their assignments rather than their humanity. Connection is sacrificed for the sake of getting the job done.

Artful leaders insist on accountability and also communicate care. They see the person in front of them not as a job title but as a human being worthy of attention. They understand that cultivating caring relationships is essential to achieving positive results. They're awake to the human potential that lives in each person they lead.

Skillful leaders understand that they can't win over the hearts and minds of those they lead unless they direct their energy and attention into building key relationships. The topic of where and how you exercise your attention is one we covered in more depth in chapter 8, The Strategic Focus Conversation. With the Relationship Conversation, we invite you to focus on the quality of your relationships and your relationship-building skills.

Are you in agreement that it's the quality of your relationships that will optimize or derail your leadership? Most leaders we coach acknowledge how critical relationships are to their success. They don't often know, however, to what extent their relationships are on- or off-track. It's not that they don't care. They simply haven't given conscious attention to a relationship-building agenda. They haven't focused on the habits they need to embrace that will enable them to rebuild damaged relationships, cultivate important ones, or accept the reality of those that are unsalvageable.

Investigating the status of your relationships is the first step to enhancing them. What's the quality of your relationships, both personal and professional? When you step back and honestly evaluate just how connected you are, what truths emerge? Without direct and thoughtful attention, damaged or precarious relationships have the potential to jeopardize the results that are only achievable through true collaboration. But how can true collaboration emerge when a leader is disconnected or at odds with her boss, direct reports, or peers?

Daniel Goleman, author of *Working with Emotional Intelligence,* suggests that how we handle ourselves in our relationships determines how well we do once we're in a given job.[2] Relationship-building skills are vital, he claims, to leadership effectiveness, and they can be developed through intentional attention. Like muscles, if we exercise them through rigorous self-assessment and practice, our leadership impact expands. If we allow them to atrophy, our influence shrinks.

If you were drawn to this chapter, you may have a gnawing sense that some of the relationships central to your success would benefit from your focused attention. Maybe you've settled into a pattern of avoiding or ignoring a particular person with whom you work closely on the heels of a difficult conversation or an unresolved conflict. Perhaps you've welcomed a new player on your leadership team but haven't devoted the necessary time to get to know him. Maybe someone's had the courage to hold up a mirror and point out the breakdowns in your relationships that are limiting your results. Your motivation for diving into this conversation is less important than the choice you have made to carefully consider the quality of your relationships and how you might improve them.

Once you've committed to the Relationship Conversation, how do you navigate your way through it? In this chapter, you'll find a road map for launching an examination of your relationships and helpful strategies for addressing breakdowns and rebuilding trust with others when necessary. And you'll create new possibilities for improved relationships and greater leadership success.

By considering our key question, "How well connected am I to those around me?" you are saying yes to serving as a catalyst in your organization. Not only will you improve the relationships that matter to you, you'll also inspire others in your organization to attend to their relationships with greater care and concern.

Phase 1: Identify Which Relationships Are On- or Off-Track

If you've ever attended a family reunion, you know there will undoubtedly be one or two relatives whom you intentionally avoid. Maybe it's Uncle Lee, who talks about himself too much, or dear Aunt Mabel, who loves to criticize other family members behind their backs. You remind yourself as you pack your suitcase to be on alert and steer clear of those relatives who simply rub you the wrong way. At the reunion picnic, you make an extra effort to seat yourself as far away from them as possible.

What's the cost of avoiding someone who you see only once every few years at a large family reunion? Probably minimal.

Change the setting from a family reunion to your organization, and the stakes get much higher. Avoiding or ignoring an individual, whether she's a peer, direct report, or boss, can jeopardize your career or minimize your influence. The strategy may take care of your discomfort or hers, but what happens when the two of you need to address a shared challenge or work together to produce a key deliverable?

If you're using your energy to avoid connecting with someone within your professional circle, then that same energy isn't available for you to use elsewhere. The discomfort or stress you feel in a troubled relationship often exacts a personal as well as a business toll. You may lose focus easily, become irritable, and even see your physical health deteriorate as a result of unaddressed relationship issues.

Identifying the people you're avoiding or ignoring is usually easy, and simply attuning yourself to the physical comfort or discomfort you feel in a colleague's presence can signal whether, for you, the relationship is on track. Later in this chapter, we'll offer you tools and strategies for influencing the status of those relationships that are off-track but matter to your leadership.

But what if your perceptions of your essential relationships don't match those of others around you? Assuming that others see and experience our relationships exactly as we do is either terribly naïve or overly optimistic. As we highlighted in chapter 2, The Impact Conversation, the higher up in the ranks you move, the more likely you are to become isolated from direct feedback about how others experience you and their relationship with you.

You may believe that your relationships with your boss, peers, and direct reports are stable and productive, but any one of those individuals may hold a very different view of your relationship. In our coaching engagements, we suggest this possible disconnect to our clients, particularly with those leaders who've received tough feedback about their interpersonal skills. We invite them to assess their key relationships from their vantage point but remind them to give equal consideration to the possibility that others may experience the relationship differently. The challenge and opportunity, we suggest, is to be genuinely curious about each important relationship and to examine it from all angles.

As Teddy Roosevelt observed more than a hundred years ago, "the most important single ingredient in the formula of success is knowing how to get along with people." Although your capacity to build strong, productive relationships is not the sole ingredient to your success, without it, you'll limit your and your organization's achievements. Our client Alex discovered how a simple assessment and a few key changes could shift the course of an important relationship and the direction of his career.

A Necessary Audit: Alex's Story

When we sat down for our first coaching conversation with Alex, we noticed how discouraged he appeared. He'd joined his company as a senior executive with years of solid experience at his back. He longed to be consulted by the company's executive leadership but found instead that conversations with his boss and other leaders felt one-sided and his expertise was largely ignored. Alex admitted that his enthusiasm for his role and confidence that he could make a meaningful difference had hit an all-time low.

Alex's dissatisfaction seemed directly connected to the quality of some of his key relationships. Important relationships with senior leaders, including with his boss, had never gotten off the ground or were locked in a holding pattern that minimized his impact. We pointed out to Alex that a leader has four sets of relationships to manage: with customers and/or external stakeholders; with other leaders above him; with colleagues; and with his direct reports. Leaders, we suggested, typically have one or two sets of relationships that they excel at managing but are not usually highly skilled in all four areas.

We asked Alex to use our Relationship Audit Worksheet (see page 191) to assess the quality of his four sets of relationships at work. He wasn't surprised to discover that his highest ratings corresponded with his customer and direct report relationships. His second highest score showed up in his relationships with his colleagues. His relationships with those above him in the company, including with his boss, received the lowest score. In stepping back and reviewing his ratings, he realized that the relationships that correlated most directly with his ability to influence the company's future—his relationships with Jane, his boss and CEO, and with other members of the executive team—were superficial at best.

He described meetings with Jane as narrow in focus and happening too irregularly for a trusting relationship with her to develop. He explained that these meetings felt more like a check-in around his key responsibilities rather than a productive back-and-forth conversation about his vision and his questions about the company's future. Likewise, his relationships with other key leaders in the company were generally friendly but shallow.

Alex recognized that his relationships with his boss and other senior executives had to deepen and improve if he was going to position himself as a leader sought out for his expertise and advice. With his intentional focus and attention, these relationships could evolve into more trusting and close connections. He realized he didn't need to stay stuck in the perspective that his contribution wasn't valued. He could actively reach out with the intention of building deeper relationships and championing his value to the company.

Equipped with this insight, Alex committed to several practices that encouraged him to extend himself toward others, particularly those higher up in the organization. He made a habit of reaching out to senior executive team members and dropping by his boss's office for informal conversations. In our coaching sessions, he practiced relaxing his body so that he would project a more at-ease and accessible presence in conversations with Jane and other senior leaders. Within a short time, Alex noticed that his mood at work had improved, his connections with those higher up in his company had strengthened, and other leaders accessed him for his opinion more frequently.

Your Turn

Take a moment now to evaluate those relationships that are central to your success. You can create a visual snapshot that captures the quality of your relationships using our Relationship Audit Worksheet. Consider these questions as you review your audit results:

1. What does your assessment of each relationship reveal? Is there one particular relationship or set of relationships that stands out with a remarkably low or high score?

2. How would it benefit the organization and your results if your lowest rated relationship or set of relationships were to improve?

RELATIONSHIP AUDIT WORKSHEET

Using a scale of 1 (low) to 10 (high), assess the quality of your relationships in each of the four key areas and total your scores. *Special Note*: In the categories of "Peers," "Direct Reports," and "Customers" (where you are evaluating more than one individual relationship), assign a general rating that reflects your overall assessment of this category of relationship.

Relationship	Trust	Respect	Connection	Total Score
Boss/Board				
Peers				
Direct Reports				
Customers				

Spending time assessing and attending to relationships can feel like "unproductive" time. But leaders we coach repeatedly share examples of the costs associated with derailed, underdeveloped, or troubled relationships in their organizations.

What's next for you after you assess the quality of your essential relationships? Completing this assessment will likely lead you to discover that certain relationships would benefit from your thoughtful attention and energy. You may feel tempted to come up with an immediate plan for addressing and improving these relationships. But before you suit up for a relationship improvement effort, it's essential to examine how you might have contributed to the relationship's status.

If the way you shift gears in your car has damaged your clutch, simply replacing the clutch won't save you from future repairs down the road. You have to adjust your driving behavior. Similarly, if you don't identify the part you play in your relationships, you may unwittingly repeat the same behaviors or hold the same mind-set that will set you up for derailment in the future. Give yourself the gift of reflection time now and learn from your past and current relationship experiences.

Turn to this chapter's next section and use the relationships you've flagged for improvement as a lens for recognizing the mind-sets or behaviors you exhibit that can damage, derail, or inhibit productive relationships. With these insights locked in, you can learn from your missteps and own their unintended consequences. Others will be more likely to view your relationship repair effort as sincere if you've reflected on and own the role you've played in any relationship breakdowns.

PHASE 2: REPAIR TRUST

Our coaching clients and our own experiences have taught us that productive and satisfying relationships all have one common ingredient: trust. When trust is present in a relationship, difficult topics can be discussed openly. When trust is absent or has eroded in a relationship, the capacity to exchange ideas candidly, problem solve, and address common concerns is lost. Unconsciously, you go into protection mode. It's not your fault. Humans are designed to crave both emotional and physical safety. When trust is low in a relationship, your brain tells you that your emotional safety is at risk. You're hardwired to protect yourself by being wary of any relationship that your brain perceives as threatening.

Take a moment to consider your web of relationships at work. Which one stands out as the most productive and satisfying? Once you've narrowed your focus on the one relationship that best fits this criterion, ask yourself, "What's the key ingredient that makes this relationship work?" What truth emerges? Most likely, trust plays a pivotal role in your most productive and satisfying relationships.

That's why we included trust as a key metric in our Relationship Audit Worksheet. Trust frees you up to blend your talents and aspirations with those of others and face the future together with energy and creativity.

What is trust and how do you know whether it's present in a relationship? Stephen M. R. Covey, consultant and author of *The Speed of Trust,* writes that "trust means confidence."[3] When you trust someone, he suggests, you have confidence in her integrity and abilities. *Merriam-Webster's Collegiate Dictionary* defines *trust* as "an assured reliance on the character, ability, strength, or truth of someone or something."

How do you define and measure trust? What does it take for you to trust someone? What might it take for someone to trust you?

When coaching our clients on the topic of trust, we often share a framework for assessing trust that appears in Charles Feltman's *The Thin Book of Trust.* Feltman suggests that trust can exist in varying degrees in a relationship based on your confidence in the other person's levels of Care, Sincerity, Competence, and Reliability.[4] Are you convinced that this person cares about your interests as much as he does about his own? Is the person honest? Do he mean what he says? Can you count on him to follow through on his commitments? Do you judge this person as competent? The more confident you are that a person embodies these attributes, the more you trust him.

When you consider your best relationship at work, how confident are you in that person's levels of Care, Sincerity, Competence, and Reliability? In your relationship with this person, how competent, caring, reliable, and honest have you been? Your most productive relationships at work reflect deep levels of trust and mirror high levels of these attributes.

Our client Jack understood that the relationship between two teams in his company had slipped into a pattern of finger-pointing and resentment that had eroded trust levels over time. Read more about his story and his efforts to consciously rebuild the trust necessary to boost his team's morale and produce the best results for his company's customers.

From Breakdown to Breakthrough: Jack's Story

In a corporate culture that tended to reinforce silos between teams, Jack's newly created team was launched to bridge a connection between the product development team responsible for software development and the client services team charged with delivering the product to customers and training them to use it successfully. Historically, the two teams had struggled to collaborate and coordinate effectively, which, not surprisingly, contributed to quality issues and product delivery delays.

For Jack and his new team to succeed, they would need to build productive relationships with both the product and client services teams and model trust-building skills for both groups of colleagues. With Jack's team's help, glitches in the product software that had the potential to damage client relationships could be addressed earlier through timely and effective back-and-forth communication with the product team.

When we began to work with Jack, he shared his concern that the relationships between his team and the product development team had deteriorated over time. He wanted to witness more trust, an improved feedback loop, and a shared problem-solving approach. Instead, what he was seeing involved a pattern of blaming, defensiveness, and a lack of responsiveness from both sides. Jack understood that his leadership approach had to shift if he wanted to see this pattern change, but he wasn't clear on the most effective next steps.

We talked about the subject of trust in relationships and the types of behaviors and mind-sets that chip away at trust over time. Jack acknowledged the types of behaviors he noticed in himself and his team members that could wipe out any gains made in building a productive and trusting relationship. He noted that his team had a habit of e-mailing product team members with problems and concerns rather than addressing them in person. Product team members invariably responded defensively—and late. Their reaction would reinforce Jack's team members' perception that the product team was disengaged, distant, and resistant to helpful feedback. Blame and resentment became the norm in the communication between both teams.

Once Jack had reflected on this situation and the ways in which his team was contributing to this unhealthy stand-off, he committed to engage his team on the topic and insist on a new communication practice that would build, rather than erode, trust. To their credit, his team members acknowledged the role their habits had played in the quality of their relationship with the product team. They agreed to assume positive intent on their colleagues' part rather than presuming the worst. His team members agreed to consult with their product team counterparts in person, either one-on-one or in a group conversation, when they encountered a software problem. This practice proved to be a simple yet powerful antidote for mistrust. Investing the energy capital needed to rebuild trust and goodwill in the relationship ensured that future problems could be addressed openly and collaboratively and with better results.

Your Turn

In a 2006 Florida State University survey, respondents indicated they would trust a total stranger more than their own boss. How is such a disappointing result possible? Take a look at our Trustworthy Leader Questionnaire and explore your level of trustworthiness. As you reflect on your results, consider the following questions:

1. Which aspect of your trustworthiness (Care, Sincerity, Competence, and Reliability) is most evident in your leadership? Which is least present?

2. Which attribute of trustworthiness do you most want to cultivate in yourself?

3. What is one concrete step you can you take immediately to increase your trustworthiness?

TRUSTWORTHY LEADER QUESTIONNAIRE

Identify those behaviors that you demonstrate routinely.

Do I Care?

- ☐ I treat every person and every role with dignity and respect.
- ☐ I seek to understand the opinions, cares, and concerns of those who work with me.
- ☐ I actually listen. Others feel seen and heard by me.
- ☐ I'm connected to what I care about.

Am I Sincere?

- ☐ I tell the truth about what I think and feel.
- ☐ My actions and body language match my words.
- ☐ My intentions and expectations are clear.
- ☐ My public and private conversations are the same.

Am I Competent?

- ☐ I have the ability and capacity to deliver on my promises and commitments.
- ☐ I'm focused on results.
- ☐ I get the right things done.
- ☐ I continually strive to get better at what I do.

Am I Reliable?

- ☐ I honor and keep my commitments to others over time.
- ☐ I have a track record of delivering results.
- ☐ I manage people's expectations well.

As Covey asserts, when trust is down, the cost of doing business goes up and the speed of delivery on commitments plummets. When mistrust is high, people in the workplace turn to self-protective strategies that often result in communication breakdowns and additional bureaucracy to compensate for the increasing level of mistrust. Low trust levels increase betrayal types of behaviors, like gossiping and sabotaging, which only reinforce and deepen suspicion. A vicious, self-perpetuating cycle of mistrust develops.

How can you prevent this cycle from infiltrating your own organizations? It starts at the level of leadership, with people like you. If you understand that building trust develops through demonstrating your Care, Sincerity, Competence, and Reliability, and you actively encourage others to cultivate the same attributes through your own example, you're off to a good start.

The trouble for many people is that they're blind to their own trust-eroding behaviors. In our combined years of coaching experienced and emerging leaders, we've never encountered one leader who intended to fracture trust. The truth is that we all engage in minor and major betrayals, occasionally intentionally but usually unconsciously, that slowly eat away at our trustworthiness and inflict discomfort or anxiety on those around us. In their book *Rebuilding Trust,* consultants Michelle and Dennis Reina suggest that betrayals result in a breach of trust that can prove difficult to overcome.[5] Trust grows over time, but mistrust can flower in an instant.

The truth is that very few, if any, people wake up in the morning determined to plant seeds of mistrust in their workplace or their relationships. If you're not mindful, though, you can slip into habits that enable mistrust to take root.

How Do I Repair Trust and Mend Relationships?

Consider your results from the Relationship Audit Worksheet that you completed earlier in this chapter. Which relationship has the lowest trust score? Why is trust low in this important relationship? What do you honestly believe it will take for this relationship to get back on track? Your assessment of the relationship and any current breakdown will help you begin to sort through what it will take to repair any damage and rebuild trust.

It may help to recall a recent instance when someone violated your trust and took helpful steps to bridge the divide between you. Perhaps your boss apologized to you for dismissing an idea you shared with her without examining it fully, or maybe your friend wrote you a note asking you to forgive him for a careless insult and pledged to be more thoughtful in the future.

Trust-repair moves like these are acts of relationship courage. They're the simple—but far from easy—steps you can take to get a relationship back on track. They are no guarantee, but they do make improvement possible. Even more important, making these moves will ensure that you've traveled the necessary distance to bring trust within reach again and recover a relationship that matters to you and your leadership.

It's useful to name these moves explicitly so that you can practice them successfully. We refer to them as the SALVE model because they have the potential to heal the wounds suffered in a damaged relationship:

- *S*tate the relationship breakdown
- *A*cknowledge and apologize for your contribution and the role you played in the relationship breakdown
- *L*isten with curiosity and nonjudgment to the other person's experience
- *V*ow to make any necessary adjustments in your behavior to rebuild trust
- *E*xpress your commitment to an improved relationship

SALVE can only serve you and move you closer to relationship recovery if you practice it with authenticity. Disingenuousness is recognizable. If you follow the right steps but your nonverbal cues suggest insincerity, the other person will sniff out your dishonesty and mistrust your intentions. So if your plan is to approach someone in your organization and practice SALVE, ask yourself now, "Do I truly acknowledge the role I played in this relationship breakdown? Do I care enough about the well-being of this relationship to admit wrongdoing and make changes in my habits, if necessary?"

Not all relationships that you flag for improvement are in jeopardy because of a specific breakdown or breach of trust. You may have rated the relationship that you identified earlier in this chapter as low simply because it's never taken off or its foundation is not solid enough to produce the results that are only possible through a more collaborative partnership.

How do you intentionally cultivate productive, high-trust relationships? By paying close attention to your own behavior, you can consciously avoid falling into trust-eroding habits. In the tool kit section of this chapter, we direct you to a Trust-Eroding Behaviors Checklist in the appendix that can help you spot any habits that undermine trust.

Developing high-trust, successful relationships requires something beyond naming trust-jeopardizing habits. It also requires *care.* If you want to position all of your relationships to deliver successful outcomes, you need to evaluate whether your presence and your behavior convey and invite a caring connection with others. Continue on in your reading and reflection, and join us in exploring this next phase in your Relationship Conversation.

PHASE 3: CREATE CARING CONNECTIONS

Recent research by neuroscientist Naomi Eisenberger and her colleagues reveals that a lack of connection with others creates symptoms analogous to those of physical pain.[6] She writes that some of the same brain regions that respond to physical pain also respond to "social pain," the emotional experience associated with feeling rejected and isolated. Not surprisingly, her research also suggests that the experience of feeling connected to others is intrinsically rewarding to the brain and nervous system. Because our early ancestors understood that social connection improved their likelihood of survival, our brains have evolved in a way that encourages us toward social attunement. In fact, when we experience a caring connection with another human being, the brain actually releases the pleasure hormone oxytocin.

Scientific research affirms what you and other leaders know to be true through your own firsthand experience and observation: establishing a caring connection with others is critical to effective leadership. Consider the role that care plays in the relationship you identified earlier as your best relationship at work. How does care show up in this relationship?

When you're open, present, and connected to others, you can better recognize what matters most to those around you. When you signal that you understand what's important to others, you're better able to mobilize and influence them. You can draw a clearer connection between what they care about and the vision and mission you hold for your organization. How well acquainted are you with what matters most to your team members? Does your presence convey care? As you read our client Cynthia's story, you'll discover how a few mindful adjustments to your presence and practice can enhance the caring connection between you and those you lead.

Expressing Care: Cynthia's Story

Our client Cynthia was blindsided by some completely unexpected difficult feedback. Her boss had expressed his concern about a number of complaints he'd received from Cynthia's team members that she had distanced herself from them and was often inaccessible. When they did get to meet with her, they pointed out, she seemed distracted. Team members noted that there'd been a shift in Cynthia's management approach, and they expressed concern that it would continue. They had always experienced her as open, engaged, and available to them in the past and missed their connection with her.

Newly promoted to a director's role in her manufacturing company, Cynthia had assumed her new responsibilities with determination and dedication. Resources were limited on her team and expectations for her IT department's results were high, so she found herself taking on the work of some of her team members out of a desire to protect them from working long hours. She cared deeply about her staff and didn't want to see them overworked.

When we first started to work with Cynthia, she had slipped into a pattern of arriving earlier and earlier at her office to accomplish what she could. Her time with team members was siphoned off by the number of hours she spent in back-to-back meetings with colleagues and executives. Her perseverance allowed her to muscle through the long hours, but she found she had little energy or attention left for interactions with her team.

She was hurt and confused when her boss, Tony, shared the feedback from her team members. She'd put her concerns for their well-being ahead of her own and couldn't understand why they would go above her to her boss to complain about her when she had taken on additional work on top of her own to lighten their load.

We launched our coaching engagement with Cynthia using a 360-degree feedback instrument and collected data from her boss, peers, and direct reports. Cynthia was open and responsive to her feedback and developed a leadership goal that focused on creating a more caring connection with her team members. She recognized that in the process of trying to protect them from longer hours and potential burnout, she'd taken on too many priorities. Focusing on these additional priorities had swallowed up any time she'd previously spent connecting with her team, both formally and informally. In an effort to take care of her staff, she'd actually distanced herself from them, and they felt disconnected and out of touch with her as a result.

Through our work together, Cynthia established some new practices that encouraged her to develop more of a visibly caring connection with her team. She allocated time to focus on the strengths of team members and acknowledged their contributions more frequently and deliberately. She paid special attention to what each of her team members needed from her in terms of contact and affirmation. With increased awareness, she was able to shape her approach to meet the unique needs of each team member and noticed that their mood and morale improved as a result. She spent more time in one-on-one contact with them, even if it was only a brief check-in. And she gave them her full attention when she did, making eye contact and extending care. Cynthia practiced letting go and delegating more of her responsibilities and discovered that her team members were open to taking on more responsibility and were eager to be challenged.

Your Turn

Intelligence and expertise are essential to effective leadership, but they are no guarantee of leadership success. Rather, it is your presence that enables you to leverage your intelligence and competence to produce desired results. Take a few moments to assess the quality of your presence and connection with those you lead:

1. On a scale of 1 to 5 (1 being low and 5 being high), how would you rate the extent to which you are present, open, and connected to those with whom you interact on a daily basis?
2. If we were to ask this same question of those with whom you interact regularly, what assessment might they give of how present, open, and connected you are on a daily basis?

Building caring connections and high-trust relationships with others isn't simply a matter of adding some new behaviors to your repertoire or removing a few unhelpful habits. As repeated experiments on the topic of credibility have proven, your trustworthiness manifests itself even more clearly in your physical presence than it does in your actions. The believability of the message that you deliver to others is influenced 7 percent by the content, 38 percent by your voice tone and tempo when you deliver the message, and 55 percent by your body language when you communicate.[7] Nearly 100 percent of your trustworthiness, it turns out, lives in your presence.

The same is true for your capacity to build a caring connection with someone else. Your ability to extend warmth and care is perceptible in your presence, from the way you stand and position yourself in relationship to others to the ease with which you can look another person in the eyes or smile.

One of the most powerful and proven methods for building trust and creating an open, present, and caring connection with others is through deep listening. Most people identify themselves as active listeners—while simultaneously viewing most other people as poor listeners! How can both experiences be true? In our experience working with and observing leaders, we've found that there's significant room for improvement in leaders' listening skills. Many leaders we coach practice a kind of listening we call *self-oriented listening*. They listen for the sake of sharing their own opinion or positions, proving others' views as wrong, or asserting their influence or authority.

Deep listening requires an *other-orientation* and more intentional effort and energy. The payoff from practicing this form of listening is a more genuine, caring connection. Bernard Ferrari, author of *Power Listening*, notes that better business decisions and results are only possible when leaders practice deep listening successfully. Ferrari champions the 80/20 rule: listen 80 percent of the time in any interaction and speak only 20 percent of the time.[8] Imagine how well conversations would go if everyone involved were to abide by this rule!

What's the formula for deep listening? How can you bring a deeper listening capability to your relationships and interactions?

The Co-Active Coaching Model developed by the Coaches Training Institute describes three different levels of listening.[9] In level 1 listening, your attention is focused on yourself. You may be listening to the words your conversation partner is speaking, but your attention is on your own reaction and on formulating a response. When you listen at level 2, you focus your attention on the other person and calculate how you can move that person forward effectively. You care and want to connect, but your intention is to move your conversation partner toward a specific agenda.

When you practice level 3 listening, you are fully present in the moment of the conversation. You listen not only to the other person but also to the interplay between you. You have a heightened awareness of interpersonal connection and suspend your agenda so you can better offer what that person needs. Listening at level 3 also enables you to express an empathy that builds relationships. Level 3 listening demands that you put aside your phone, turn off your e-mail, and be entirely present to the person in front of you.

Take a moment now to step back and reflect on the quality of your listening. What level of listening do you typically practice, and how is it helping or hurting your relationships? If you want to intentionally become a more open, present, and connected leader and cultivate caring connections with those around you, listening at level 3 in more of your interactions will serve you well.

As you bring a new level of resolve to listening and communicating care, you will radically alter the way you engage and connect with others. Even small, thoughtful adjustments to your nonverbal presence and habits will have a big impact on your relationships and ensure that your key relationships are built on a foundation of trust.

THE RELATIONSHIP CONVERSATION: KEY TAKEAWAYS

The Relationship Conversation invited you to step back and ask yourself a vital question: "How well connected am I to those around me?" As you reflected on this key inquiry, we encouraged you to thoughtfully assess your key relationships. You discovered which ones are on track and which ones are derailed and require your attention. With this awareness in mind, you were better positioned to examine the level of trust you've built with various stakeholders and acknowledge and own some of the trust-eroding habits you've slipped into unconsciously.

Your leadership impact will now expand because you honestly assessed the quality of your connections and your ability to be open, present, and connected to those whom you want to influence. Having engaged in the Relationship Conversation, you'll become an even more influential and trusted leader in your organization: someone who wins over the hearts and the minds of those you lead.

The Relationship Conversation: What's Next?

Coaching Assignments for Leveraging Your Learning

Is the Relationship Conversation particularly critical for you? The following list of Actions, Practices, and Resources is a tool kit for engaging more deeply in this important Missing Conversation.

Action Steps

- Ask others around you to complete the Trustworthy Leader Questionnaire on your behalf so you can learn how others view you and your credibility as a trustworthy leader. Compare their assessments to your own. Target a dimension of your trustworthiness (Care, Sincerity, Competence, and Reliability) for improvement and make some specific commitments regarding actions you'll take and habits you'll change that will strengthen your credibility in that dimension.
- Complete the Trust-Eroding Behaviors Checklist (see page 219 in the appendix) or ask a trusted neutral observer to complete it for you so you can increase your awareness of those behaviors you engage in that chip away at trust in your relationships.
- Use the following recommended questions to engage your team members and/or other important stakeholders in a "State of Our Union" conversation about the status of your relationship. Remember to listen openly and with curiosity and understand that asking these questions means that you are truly interested in learning about how this person experiences you and your impact and that you are willing to make needed adjustments to improve the relationship.
    - What about how we are working together currently helps you operate successfully in your role?
    - What about how we are working together is getting in the way of your effectiveness or success?
    - If you could make one change to how I interact and/or work with you, what would you want that one change to be?
- Recruit a neutral outsider to be an observer of you when you are in meetings with others in your organization. Ask your observer to note how much of the talking you are doing in these conversations and whether you appear to be listening effectively.

Ongoing Practices

- Sharpen your ability to read others by routinely watching a television show or a movie with the sound off so that you can observe, study, and form assessments of the mood, emotions, and well-being of people based solely on their nonverbals. This practice will strengthen your muscles of observation and attunement to others, which will help build your capacity for connection.

- On a routine basis, acknowledge the strengths and contributions of each person with whom you work and express your gratitude with a written thank-you (e-mails are OK, but a written note is even better).
- Go on a fifteen-minute Care Tour in your workplace on a regular basis. Greet people by name and extend a caring connection to them.

Suggested Resources

Leadership and Self-Deception: Getting Out of the Box by the Arbinger Institute: Berrett-Koehler, 2010.

Power Listening: Mastering the Most Critical Business Skill of All by Bernard T. Ferrari: Penguin Group, 2012.

Rebuilding Trust in the Workplace: Seven Steps to Renew Confidence, Commitment, and Energy by Dennis S. Reina and Michelle L. Reina: Berrett-Koehler, 2010.

Speed of Trust: The One Thing That Changes Everything by Stephen M. R. Covey: Free Press, 2006.

CONCLUSION

Do you make regular visits to yourself?

—Rumi

"Do the people you coach *really* change?" a friend asked us on a recent neighborhood walk. Her tone betrayed a hint of skepticism as she raised a question we've been asked many times before. We responded without equivocation, "Yes, but only if they really want to." Our clients have taught us that the kind of change that is sustainable over time only comes with tremendous effort and desire. After all, change threatens the status quo, and human beings are designed to preserve things just as they are.

The leaders with whom we work have taught us that real transformation is possible when our desire to become more effective overcomes our tendency to remain the same. Their stories and successes inspired us to write *Missing Conversations* as an invitation to transform for leaders like you.

When you picked up this book, you said yes to this invitation. You know better than to wait for others around you to make adjustments or hope that situations will get better on their own. You're the kind of leader who recognizes that better results await you, those you lead, and your organization when *you* change. Perhaps you're disciplined and dedicated to self-improvement by nature. Maybe recent breakdowns have caused you to question and reconsider your current leadership practices. Either way, we've written this book with you in mind.

Leading others is exciting but demanding work. It may be a luxury for you to allow yourself the time and space to pause and reflect. If you've given yourself permission to read this book and connect it to your leadership, you've made an investment in your development that will impact the quality of your leadership immediately.

You can only lead others skillfully when you manage yourself wisely. *Missing Conversations* developed out of our heartfelt aspiration to provide reflections, stories, and recommendations that expand your wisdom and support your transformation. Our hope is that *Missing Conversations* has engaged you in the nine reflections that are essential to your self-awareness, satisfaction, and success as a leader. If you've explored any or all of these nine conversations with yourself, they're no longer missing. If you've implemented new practices or taken new actions as a result of what you've read and reflected on, you're on the pathway toward accessing your leadership potential. And, like the leaders who've inspired us, may your commitment to transformation encourage those you lead to learn and develop, too.

APPENDIX

Sample 360-Degree Feedback Questions

1. What would you say are this leader's greatest strengths? What specific things does he or she do particularly well that you appreciate?
2. Please share one example of a time when this leader was at his or her best and was able to make a meaningful difference for you or those around you. What did this leader do, and how did he or she add value?
3. How well does this leader create and communicate organizational clarity? Do you have a shared understanding of your organization's mission, vision, values, strategic priorities, goals, roles, and the game plan for achieving them? How might he or she do even better here?
4. How well do you understand this leader's role in the organization?
5. Can you identify one or two of his or her areas of weakness? How well does he or she manage areas of weakness?
6. To what extent does this leader strike a good balance between stepping in to give guidance and support and stepping out to let others do their jobs?
7. What does this leader do that builds trust with you and others? What does he or she do (or not do) that might erode trust with you or others?
8. What is one thing that this leader might not see about himself or herself (either positive or negative) that, if the leader could see it, would help him or her to have an even greater impact?
9. How would you describe this leader's presence in meetings with colleagues or clients? What might he or she do to strengthen or improve his or her presence?

10. In light of everything we've discussed, what is the most important change this leader could make to be more effective?

Common Moods and Their Impact

Anxiety

- Supported by an underlying belief or story that the world is unsafe or that bad things are likely to happen, along with significant doubt about our ability to deal with them
- Characterized by shallow or restricted breathing (breathing from the chest instead of the abdomen), raised shoulders, and closed chest (shoulders come in to protect our heart and vital organs)
- Predisposes us to play it safe, avoid risks, and protect the status quo; also contributes to heightened reactivity

Resentment

- Supported by an underlying belief or story that we have been treated unfairly or disrespected
- Characterized by tension in the eyes, jaw, or shoulders
- Predisposes us to blame others for our situation, to point fingers, and to avoid looking at our own behavior

Resignation

- Supported by an underlying belief or story that there's nothing we can do to affect our situation, a "why bother?" mentality, and a sense of powerlessness
- Characterized by slumped posture, curving of our spine and shoulders, and diminished vertical line
- Predisposes us to become cynical and skeptical; keeps us from seeing possibilities or from exploring new ways of doing things

Optimism

- Supported by an underlying belief or story that exciting possibilities exist and that we are capable of making them happen
- Characterized by an open chest, relaxed shoulders, a "tall" spine, and an energetic presence

- Predisposes us to take risks, to see and explore possibilities, and to stay the course in the midst of breakdowns or setbacks

Curiosity

- Supported by an underlying belief or story that the world is an interesting place, that we are capable learners, and that others are as well
- Characterized by a relaxed overall posture
- Predisposes us to engage with the world and those around us, to ask questions, to experiment with new ideas or solutions ("I wonder what would happen if we tried it this way?"), to suspend judgment, and to create new possibilities

Lightheartedness

- Supported by an underlying belief or story that the world is a joyful place, that we are deserving of joy, and that others are as well
- Characterized by an open chest, relaxed shoulders, soft eyes, and a lightness in our hands, legs, and feet
- Predisposes us to find humor, to engage playfully with others, and to find perspective in the midst of breakdowns or setbacks

Impact Statement and Actions Worksheet

Name: Date:

Commitment	Key Indicators*	Actions to Take**	Essential Practices***
I am committed to . . .			

*How will you know you're making progress toward your commitment?
**What actions will help you advance toward your commitment?
***What practices will support you in achieving your commitment?

Sample Impact Statement and Actions Worksheet

Commitment	Key Indicators*	Actions to Take**	Essential Practices***
I am committed to being a caring leader who helps people leverage their strengths.	My team members function well in roles that align with their strengths.	Use the Strengths Finder 2.0 with my team.	Meet weekly with each team member one on one. Write at least one note of appreciation/week to a team member.

THE CENTERING PRACTICE

(adapted with permission from *The Leadership Dojo* by Richard Strozzi-Heckler)

Centering is a physical practice designed to build your capacity to be open, present, and grounded. As you introduce and sustain this simple practice, you will become less reactive and more of a calm presence for those you lead. Your well-being will improve as you attune to your body, relax any tension that you're holding in your muscles, align yourself three-dimensionally, and connect with what you care about most.

The practice happens in two phases and can be done either standing or sitting, although we recommend standing as you familiarize yourself with the practice.

You'll bring your energy and attention to two different but connected elements of your presence: the level of relaxation and ease in your muscles and the alignment of your body in three distinct dimensions (length, width, and depth).

Begin by standing in a relaxed posture with your eyes open and your gaze resting on a spot across the room.

Step 1: Sweep your attention from the crown of your head to the toes of your feet, paying special attention to any area of your body where you sense you are holding tension. Usual suspects include the area around your eyes; the jaw, upper shoulders, neck, and back; the belly; and the thighs. As you tune in to your body, alert yourself to any areas that are contracted and gently release them. When you let your skeleton do the work of holding your body erect, your muscles can relax and let go. As a result, you project a more relaxed and open presence to others.

Step 2: Center your physical body as well as your energy in three dimensions: *length, width,* and *depth.*

Center in Your Length

To center in your length, let your attention focus on your feet. Sense the connection between your feet and the floor. Imagine this connection extending to the earth beneath you. Then, allow your attention to sweep from your feet through the center of your body alongside your spine. As it emerges from the crown of your head, stand fully upright and embody your dignity.

Center in Your Width

To center in your width, shift your weight between your left and right foot until you find that place precisely between the two. Imagine yourself extending and expanding out into the world around you. Sense your connection with others and the space that is uniquely yours to inhabit. When you are centered in your width, you are aware of yourself in relationship to the world around you.

Center in Your Depth

To center in your depth, allow your weight to shift forward and backward until you find that place in between the two where your weight is evenly distributed on your feet. Rather than shifting forward physically and falling into the future or leaning backward and retreating from life, find the balance that allows you to be perfectly present in the here and now. When you are centered in your depth, you are in touch with your self-sufficiency and are fully present in the moment.

Center in Your Purpose and Potential

Place a hand on your physical center, that place on your body just below the belly button. As you make contact with your physical center, remind yourself what and whom you care about. Recall your intentions and commitments. Ground yourself in your purpose.

The practice of Centering can be done in five minutes or in thirty seconds. The amount of time you spend Centering is less important than the quality of your attention when you're in the practice. You'll notice the benefits the more frequently you practice. When you engage in this practice routinely, your nervous system will develop a greater capacity to recover from triggering events or people with ease, and you will project a more confident, grounded, and open presence to those around you.

Triggers Worksheet

What people and/or circumstances triggered reactivity in me today?	How did I experience reactivity in my body? (sensations and location in my body)	How did I behave when I was triggered?	What calms me down when I'm triggered? (activities/ practices)

Wheel of Well-Being

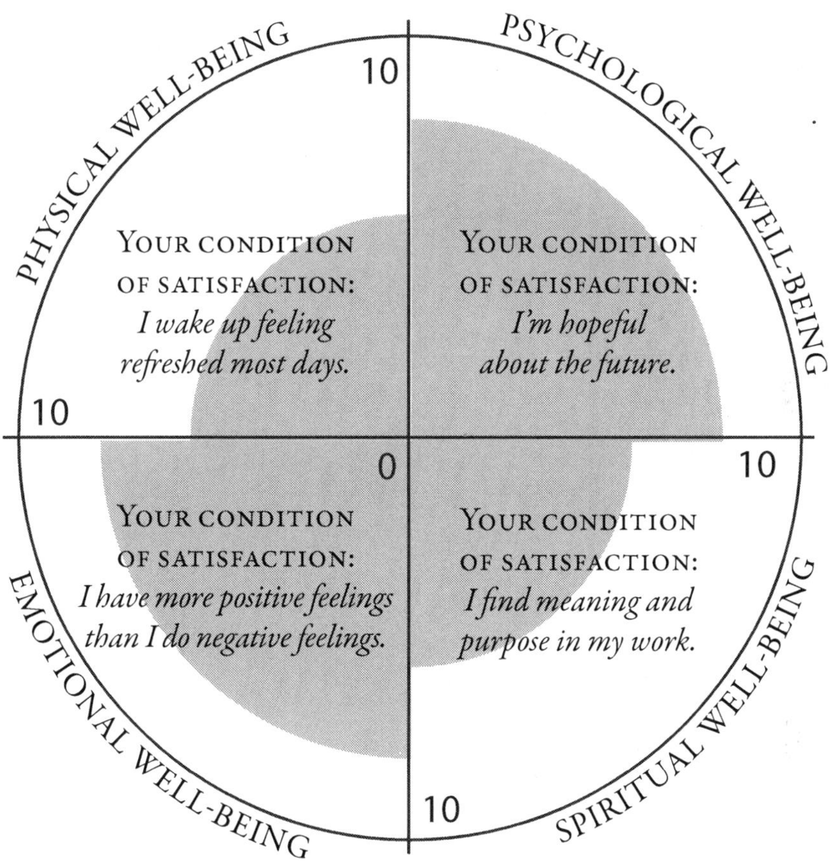

The four sections in the Wheel of Well-Being represent the four different dimensions of your overall well-being: Body, Mind, Heart, and Spirit. Each of these dimensions has space for you to insert a key "condition of satisfaction" that you associate with that particular dimension of your well-being.

Directions for Completing the Wheel:

Reflect on each dimension of your well-being and identify a key indicator for it. For example, a key indicator for you in the dimension of Physical Well-Being might be "I wake up most days feeling refreshed."

From 0 (center of the wheel) to 10 (the outside edge of the wheel), rank how well you're meeting each indicator by drawing a line to create a new outer edge. The new perimeter represents the Wheel of Your Well-Being. (See our sample Wheel on the previous page as a guide.)

Your Wheel ratings can serve as a compass for you as you identify the dimension of your well-being that needs your attention first. The Wheel can also help you reassess and track any progress in your well-being as you take action to improve one or more dimensions.

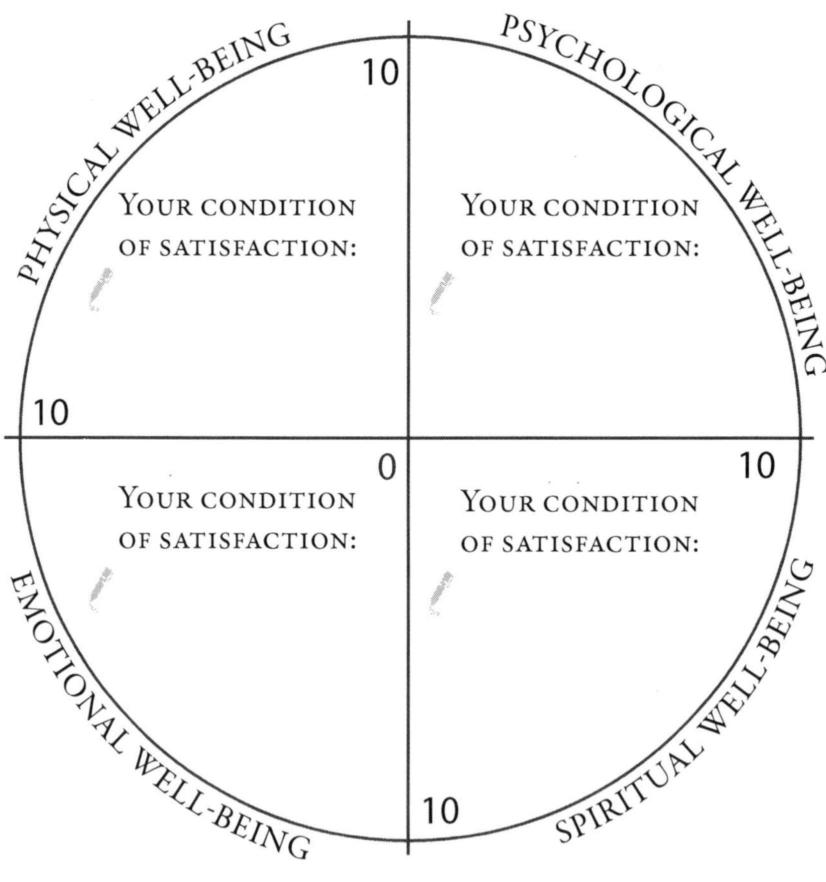

Trust-Eroding Behaviors Checklist

- ☐ I regularly cancel my scheduled appointments with team members or others with whom I work.
- ☐ I don't conduct my performance evaluations of others on a timely basis.
- ☐ I don't prepare sufficiently for the performance evaluations and/or performance conversations I have with others.
- ☐ I interrupt people frequently when in conversation.
- ☐ I tend to dominate the conversations I'm in with others.
- ☐ I delay responding to others' requests for information and/or support.
- ☐ I "sit" on others' work routinely, impacting their ability to fulfill on their commitments.
- ☐ I correct others' work frequently and return their work product with substantive rewrites and/or changes.
- ☐ I avoid having the tough conversations with others about their performance and/or impact.
- ☐ I talk about others behind their backs.
- ☐ I take credit for others' work publicly.
- ☐ I "protect" my team from overwork by taking on their work rather than delegating it to them completely.
- ☐ I consistently arrive late for meetings.
- ☐ I routinely dismiss and/or discount others' ideas.
- ☐ I sometimes hoard important job-related information from others.
- ☐ I cover up my mistakes rather than owning them and taking responsibility.
- ☐ I allow others to practice rude or inappropriate behavior without confronting them.
- ☐ I miss deadlines repeatedly and/or don't fulfill on my commitments.
- ☐ I give some individuals at work the "silent treatment."

NOTES

Introduction

1. Bob Dunham, founder of the Institute for Generative Leadership, first introduced us to the concept of Missing Conversations in his course Coaching for Excellence in Organizations (CEO), offered in partnership with Newfield Network.

Chapter 1

1. Sheryl Sandberg, *Lean In: Women, Work, and the Will to Lead* (New York: Alfred A. Knopf, 2013).
2. Lao Tzu (Laozi), *Tao Te Ching: Classic of the Way and Virtue,* 2014, compiled by Michael P. Garofalo (Red Bluff, CA: Gushen Grove Notebooks, 2014).
3. Rick Hanson, *The Buddha's Brain: The Practical Neuroscience of Happiness, Love and Wisdom* (Oakland, CA: New Harbinger, 2009).
4. Barbara Frederickson, *Positivity: Top-Notch Research Reveals the 3-to-1 Ratio That Will Change Your Life* (New York: Crown, 2009).
5. Walter Isaacson, *Steve Jobs* (New York: Simon and Schuster, 2011), 328.
6. David Whyte, *The Heart Aroused: Poetry and the Preservation of the Soul in Corporate America* (New York: Doubleday, 1994), 265.

Chapter 2

1. Jennifer Robison, "Turning Around Employee Turnover," *Gallup Business Journal,* May 8, 2008.

2. Ronald A. Heifetz and Marty Linsky, *Leadership on the Line: Staying Alive through the Dangers of Leading* (Boston: Harvard Business Review Press, 2002), 51–54.

CHAPTER 3

1. Paul Ekman, *Emotions Revealed: Recognizing Faces and Feelings to Improve Communication and Emotional Life* (New York: Henry Holt, 2003).
2. Bob Duggan and Jim Moyer, *Resilient Leadership: Navigating the Hidden Chemistry of Organizations* (Philadelphia: Infinity, 2009).
3. Richard Strozzi-Heckler and instructors at the Strozzi Institute introduced us to this concept of conditioned tendencies that live in the human nervous system (fight, flight, freeze, and appease) and the importance of developing awareness of these tendencies in our body to exercise greater choice about our behavior.
4. Jeffrey M. Schwartz and Rebecca Gladding, *You Are Not Your Brain: The 4-Step Solution for Changing Bad Habits, Ending Unhealthy Thinking, and Taking Control of Your Life* (New York: Penguin Group, 2011).
5. Richard J. Davidson and Sharon Begley, *The Emotional Life of Your Brain: How Its Unique Patterns Affect the Way You Think, Feel, and Live—and How You Can Change Them* (New York: Penguin Group, 2012).
6. Pattakos, Alex, *Prisoners of Our Thoughts: Viktor Frankl's Principles for Discovering Meaning in Life and Work* (San Francisco: Berrett-Koehler Publishers, 2010).

CHAPTER 4

1. "Capacity," http://www.macmillandictionary.com/us/dictionary/american/capacity.
2. "What Is Capacity?," http://www.BusinessDictionary.com/definition/capacity.html.

3. "Capacity," http://google-dictionary.so8848.com/meaning?word=capacity.
4. Ellen Galinsky, *Overwork in America: When the Way We Work Becomes Too Much* (New York: Families and Work Institute, 2004), 1–3.
5. Bob Dunham, "Managing Capacity, Managing Promises, Building the Future," unpublished white paper.
6. The idea of making a Capacity Declaration was introduced to us by Bob Dunham, founder of the Institute for Generative Leadership.
7. Jeffrey A. Miller, *The Anxious Organization: Why Smart Companies Do Dumb Things* (Tempe, AZ: Facts on Demand Press, 2008), 61.

Chapter 5

1. John J. Ratey, *Spark: The Revolutionary Science of Exercise and the Brain* (New York: Little, Brown, 2008).
2. David K. Randall, "Decoding the Science of Sleep," *Wall Street Journal,* August 3, 2012.
3. Richard Strozzi-Heckler, *The Leadership Dojo: Build Your Foundation as an Exemplary Leader* (Berkeley, CA: Frog, 2007).
4. Dan Siegel, *Mindsight: The New Science of Transformation* (New York: Bantam Books, 2011).
5. Chade-Meng Tan, *Search Inside Yourself: The Unexpected Path to Achieving Success, Happiness (and World Peace)* (New York: HarperCollins, 2012).

Chapter 6

1. We were first introduced to the idea of an inside-out approach to career development when we participated in a course taught by Fern Gorin, founder of the Career and Life Purpose Institute.
2. Best-selling author Marcus Buckingham has strongly advocated for a focus on personal strengths as the most effective way to unleash potential. Buckingham has been the main proponent of redefining strengths as those activities that give you energy and that strength-

en you, as opposed to simply those things you are good at doing.

3. Tom Rath, *Strengths Finder 2.0* (New York: Gallup Press, 2007), iii.
4. Joseph Jaworski, *The Inner Path of Leadership* (San Francisco: Berrett-Koehler, 2011), 3.
5. Ariel and Shya Kane, *Working on Yourself Doesn't Work: A Book about Instantaneous Transformation* (New York: Ask Productions, 1999).

Chapter 7

1. Martin E. P. Seligman, *Learned Optimism: How to Change Your Mind and Your Life* (New York: Vintage Books, 2006).
2. Justin Menkes, *Better under Pressure: How Great Leaders Bring Out the Best in Themselves and Others* (Boston: Harvard Business Review Press, 2011).
3. Jim Collins, *Good to Great: Why Some Companies Make the Leap and Others Don't* (New York: HarperCollins, 2001), 86.
4. Jeff Chadiha, "Jim Harper Is a Genuine Success," ESPN NFL, November 2011, http://espn.go.com.
5. Daniel H. Pink, *Drive: The Surprising Truth about What Motivates Us* (New York: Penguin Group, 2009).
6. Edwin H. Friedman, *A Failure of Nerve: Leadership in the Age of the Quick Fix* (New York: Seabury Books, 2007), 11.

Chapter 8

1. Maggie Jackson, *Distracted: The Erosion of Attention and the Coming Dark Age* (New York: Prometheus Books, 2008), 17.
2. Linda Stone on Continuous Partial Attention, http://www.lindastone.net.
3. "Multitasking: Switching Costs," March 20, 2006, http://www.apa.org/research/action/multitask.aspx.
4. Chris Woolston, "Multi-tasking and Stress," March 11, 2014, http://www.consumer.healthday.com.

5. Edward M. Hallowell, *CrazyBusy: Overstretched, Overbooked, and About to Snap! Strategies for Handling Your Fast-Paced Life* (New York: Ballantine Books, 2007), 137.
6. Linda Stone, "The Connected Life: From Email Apnea to Conscious Computing," http://www.huffingtonpost.com/linda-stone/email-apnea-screen-apnea-_b_1476554.html.

CHAPTER 9

1. James M. Kouzes and Barry Z. Posner, *The Leadership Challenge* (San Francisco: John Wiley, 2007), 233.
2. Daniel Goleman, *Working with Emotional Intelligence* (New York: Bantam Books, 1998).
3. Stephen M. R. Covey, *The Speed of Trust* (New York: Free Press, 2006), 5.
4. Charles Feltman, *The Thin Book of Trust* (Bend, OR: Thin Book of Publishing Co., 2009).
5. Dennis Reina and Michelle Reina, *Rebuilding Trust in the Workplace* (San Francisco: Berrett-Koehler, 2010).
6. Naomi Eisenberger and George Kohlrieser, "Lead with Your Heart, Not Just Your Head," *Harvard Business Review Blog Network,* November 16, 2012.
7. Albert Mehrabian, *Silent Messages: Implicit Communication of Emotions and Attitudes* (Boston: Wadsworth, 1980).
8. Bernard T. Ferrari, *Power Listening* (New York: Penguin Group, 2012).
9. We both received our initial coach training through the Coaches Training Institute (http://www.thecoaches.com), where we were introduced to the concept of listening at levels 1, 2, and 3.

ACKNOWLEDGMENTS

Bridgette's acknowledgments:

As we said in our introduction, leadership is not for the faint of heart. I have also learned firsthand that writing a book is not for the faint of heart. *Missing Conversations* was made possible by the generous support of our colleagues, family members, and friends, who never lost faith in us, even when it seemed like we would never finish this book! I am especially grateful for the love and support of my husband and three children. Thank you for believing in me.

I became a coach because my first mentor, Pam Walsh, introduced me to the profession long before anyone knew what it was. Thanks to her, I found my life's work—coaching leaders to become a more inspired and effective presence in their organizations. A special debt of gratitude goes to each and every client with whom I have had the privilege of working; you know who you are. Two long-term clients, Jonathan Terrell and Scott Gilbert, have been particularly impactful in the life of my business and in providing inspiration for this book. Thank you both.

The idea to write this book was born while I attended Bob Dunham's brilliant course, Coaching for Excellence in Organizations. That idea became a commitment that I embodied as a result of attending Richard Strozzi's Somatic Coach certification program. Many thanks to both of them for their deep wisdom and masterful teaching. Two other mentors and wise teachers in their own right, Jim Moyer and Bob Duggan, have been instrumental guides and unfailing supporters along the way. Thank you to Tom Serena and AnaLia Medina, who generously read drafts of the entire manuscript and offered invaluable feedback and encouragement.

Lastly, a heartfelt thank-you to my coauthor, Heather Jelks. She made writing this book fun and rewarding. Without her generosity of spirit, skillful collaboration, and deep insight, this book never would have happened.

HEATHER'S ACKNOWLEDGMENTS:

Completing this book would never have been possible without the unwavering support of my family, who both championed and challenged me to follow this dream through to completion. My mother, father, and brother rallied behind this project from the beginning, and the loving encouragement my husband and children provided sustained me when I needed it most. I am particularly grateful to all the courageous and talented leaders with whom I've worked over the years. Their eagerness to evolve and grow inspired me to write this book. We went "public" with our goal to write this book while enrolled in the somatic coach certification program with Richard Strozzi-Heckler and the Strozzi Institute community. With the generous guidance of our teachers and fellow coaches in the program, our goal to write a meaningful book became an embodied commitment.

A special thanks to clients, colleagues, and dear friends who inspired me toward the finish line, especially Jim Moyer, Bob Duggan, Sabrina Detlef, Jennifer Procopio Wright, Brenda Rinaman, Sharon Armstrong, Catherine Joyce, Jackie Ginley, Katherine Grubbs, and Heidi Kotzian. Gifted leaders like Lisa Banks, Tim Rinaman, Vince Wolfington, and Bill Magner read all or portions of our manuscript and offered valuable feedback and encouragement. A heartfelt thank-you to the team at StyleMatters whose expertise guided us toward publication.

And most importantly, I am indebted to my coauthor, Bridgette Theurer, for inviting me to collaborate with her on *Missing Conversations.* Her skill, generosity, and grace have enriched me, and I'm a better coach and human being for knowing her.

ABOUT THE AUTHORS

Bridgette Theurer has more than twenty-five years of experience coaching and training individuals and teams around the world. Her clients have included senior executives, managers, and other professionals from a wide variety of organizations, including Marriott, Sodexho USA, Lockheed-Martin, George Mason University, the FDA, and Asbury, as well as numerous small businesses and startups.

In addition to her experience as an executive coach, she has worked extensively in human resources and organizational development, both as a corporate trainer and as an independent management consultant. She is a certified career coach and has completed training programs with both the Coaches Training Institute (CTI) and the Institute of Generative Leadership (attending their Coaching for Excellence in Organizations course, or CEO). She is part of a team of coaches tapped to design and facilitate a twelve-month Leadership Development Program for the FDA. An avid lifelong learner, she recently became certified as a somatic coach through the Strozzi Institute.

Bridgette is president and founder of ClearCompass, a corporate coaching company, and lives with her husband in the Washington, D.C., metropolitan area. Her proudest accomplishment to date is raising three children who have grown into remarkable and loving adults.

Heather O'Neill Jelks is the president of Nautilus Coaching & Consulting, LLC, an executive coaching and consulting company dedicated to the development of masterful leaders. She has more than twenty years of experience in the fields of organization and leadership development with a background in leadership coaching, facilitation, conflict resolution, and training design and delivery. An avid runner and mindfulness meditation practitioner, Heather introduces her clients to leadership concepts and best practices that cultivate resilience, wisdom, and well-being. Her coaching clients include both emerging and experienced leaders in business, health care, the federal government, and the non-profit sector, including the U.S. Food and Drug Administration, Morgan Stanley/Smith Barney, and Georgetown University Hospital.

Heather is an accredited executive coach trained through the Coaches Training Institute. She also holds a Somatic Coach certification through the Strozzi Institute. She graduated from Georgetown University, completed a master's degree in organization development from the American University/NTL program, and holds a graduate certificate in conflict resolution from George Mason University. Heather has also trained in mindfulness-based stress reduction with Jon Kabat-Zinn.

She lives in the Washington, D.C., area with her husband and seventeen-year-old twins.

To contact the authors or to learn more about the training and coaching programs they offer, you may visit www.missingconversations.com

Made in the USA
Columbia, SC
26 April 2018